Between Mother and Daughter

Between Mother and Daughter

Sheila Schuller Coleman

Fleming H. Revell Company
Old Tappan, New Jersey

Unless otherwise identified, Scripture quotations are based on the King James Version of the Bible.

Scripture verses identified TLB are taken from *The Living Bible,* copyright 1971 by Tyndale House Publishers, Wheaton, IL. Used by permission.

Scripture quotations identified RSV are from the Revised Standard Version of the Bible, copyrighted 1946, 1952, © 1971 and 1973.

"Jesus and His Disciples" by Edna St. Vincent Millay from COLLECTED POEMS, Harper & Row. Copyright 1954 by Norma Millay Ellis.

Quotation from THE COURAGE OF CAROL, by Robert and Arvella Schuller
COPYRIGHT © 1978 Robert H. Schuller
Published by Harvest House Publishers, Eugene, Oregon 97402

Library of Congress Cataloging in Publication Data

Coleman, Sheila Schuller.
  Between mother and daughter.
  1. Coleman, Sheila Schuller.   2. Mothers and daughters.
3. Family—Religious life.
I. Title.
HQ755.85.C64   306.8'743   82-528
ISBN 0-8007-1304-4   AACR2

Copyright © 1982 by Sheila Schuller Coleman
Published by Fleming H. Revell Company
All rights reserved
Printed in the United States of America

Contents

Introduction, by Robert Schuller 7
Introduction, by Arvella Schuller 9
1. Mannequins, Models, and Mothers 13

Part I: Between Mother and Daughter—Modeling 27

2. Free to Be—You and Me 29
3. Responsibility? or Response-Ability? 38
4. Accept! Accept! Accept! 50

Part II: Between Mother and Daughter—Friendship 59

5. When a Mother Is a Friend 61
6. Silence—Is It Always Golden? 71
7. Dream a Little Dream With Me 83

Part III: Between Mother and Daughter—Love 97

8. Love Expects and Accepts 99
9. Love Respects 110
10. Love Reflects 126
11. The Supreme Model of Love 141

Much of the credit for the
warm, fun-filled relationship that
mom and I enjoy goes to my mom's
mom and the love and laughter that
she so graciously modeled.
Consequently I have chosen to dedicate
this book to Mrs. Louis DeHaan.
Thanks grandma, we love you.

Introduction

Few sights are more inspirational for a husband and father to behold than a creative relationship between his wife and his daughter.

I'll never know how much inspiration I owe to the positive emotional climate in my home. I am surely convinced that the positive personality of my first and only wife and the mother of my five children is as important as any other contributing element to the happiness and success I have known personally and professionally.

I'm delighted that my daughter Sheila has successfully communicated in these pages a rare, rich, remarkable, rewarding relationship between herself and her mom.

Principles that could be applied to other homes are contained in these pages.

I offer this strong word. Decide—before you read the first page—that you will believe what you read here! The temptation will be to only receive the message halfheartedly. It may be hard for you to believe that Sheila's mother is "really that good." Or that the relationship is "really that wonderful and beautiful." Cynicism is so pervasive in our society that there will be those who would not believe this book unless it contained some negative, critical, cynical stains on what is a very precious and almost pure mother-daughter relationship.

My warning then is: Be careful. You probably will be tempted to react with the negative suspicion, "It's too good to be true!"

My promise is: It's true! And it can be for you, too!

Thank you, Sheila, for writing the book. Thank you, Arvella, for living the kind of life that made this book possible.

ROBERT H. SCHULLER

Introduction

"You have a daughter!" the doctor's voice proudly proclaimed, as I heard the tiny cry of our firstborn child, Sheila.

Frightened and awed by this squirming bundle, my twenty-three-year-old husband and I (I was twenty-one) began the adventure of being parents. Now, three daughters, a son, and nearly four grandchildren later, we still are enjoying the exciting adventure of parenting.

Sheila was our pioneer in every way. She was our experiment, and we are immensely proud of her. Always curious, Sheila was ready to try something new or strange to her. She had and still has a tremendous capacity to enjoy life and to learn from the many projects jammed into a day.

I knew she would move ahead with tremendous responsibility the day I met my three-year-old at the top of the stairs, carrying her two-week-old baby brother, Bobby, in her arms. From that day on, she has always been a few steps ahead of me.

In these pages you will find mature wisdom and a generous heart—qualities that all adults hope someday to achieve—and the author, Sheila, has accomplished this in just a few years.

Her proud mother,
ARVELLA SCHULLER

Between Mother and Daughter

1

Mannequins, Models, and Mothers

My face felt hot with shame, despite the sharp winter wind that whipped across the Michigan campus. I couldn't believe my ears: me, using such profanity! Sure, many of the girls at college talked that way, but I didn't want to.

Lately I had noticed that my choice of words included some of my friends' vocabulary. Although this bothered me, I seemed unable to shake it.

On this day, however, as I heard myself speak, an image of my mother, over three thousand miles away, flashed clearly before me. I saw her beautiful mouth start to form the words I had just uttered. Vehemently, my mind vomited the idea. The choice was clear. I didn't want to talk like the girls I lived with; I wanted to be like my mother. Her strong influence instantly cured me of a potentially ugly habit.

Never again did I let a word of profanity cross my lips. Rarely did one even enter my thoughts. At that moment, mother became my living, conscious model. Since that time, if ever I have been in doubt as to what to say, think, or do in a critical situation, I have always stopped and tried to imagine what mom would do.

Modeling is the crux of mother-daughter bonds.

The success of these relationships seems to hinge upon the modeling process between a mother, the model, and her daughter, the observer.

Let me illustrate. Mom and I have a favorite pastime: lunch at Bullocks, a store where fashion shows are daily presented in the dining room. As we dine on cool salads and refreshing iced tea, beautiful models wander among the patrons, displaying their finery. The patrons comment on every dress or suit. Sometimes the color's a luscious shade, just perfect for fair complexions. A distinctive style may attract attention; but other times a patron may consider an outfit too frilly, too tailored, or too baggy. Always, one dress is perfect for a particular patron, and you hear her say, "Oh, that's beautiful! I'd love to have *that* dress."

In spite of her attempts at objectivity, the model influences viewers. If she models a dress beautifully and gracefully displays the flow of the gown or confidently strides down the aisle in her neat-fitting suit, the potential buyer is impressed. But if she has a bad day and trips, the patrons see nothing but her embarrassment.

On the way to the Tea Room, one must pass several mannequins, carefully positioned throughout the store. They stand stiffly, clothes hanging lifelessly, but draped as attractively as possible, to draw the shopper's attention to the outfit's color, style, and total look. These lifeless women never have to fear stumbling or any other hazard, for they will never take a single step to promote their outfits. Mannequins are silent, perfect models.

Several months ago, while mom and I lunched at

Mannequins, Models, and Mothers

Bullocks, it suddenly dawned on me that there are actually three kinds of models: (1) lifeless mannequins; (2) models whose day is ruined by an embarrassing trip or stumble; (3) and the graceful queens of fashion, those who demand the attention and applause. I realized that just like models and shoppers, mothers display their qualities, values, and beliefs; the daughters, like the potential buyers, observe, evaluate, and choose. Most important, the daughters' choices will always be enhanced—or unfortunately, at times, blurred—by the mothers' presentation.

Let's take a closer look at these comparisons.

The Mannequins

The mannequin just stands there. It's easy to see what she's wearing, and the clothes always look great on her perfect figure. But you have a hard time imagining how they'd look on you. How many times have you seen a dress that looked great on the mannequin, but was a bitter disappointment in the dressing room? The fault doesn't always lie in one's figure. Sometimes the mannequins just aren't built realistically (or so I'd like to think).

Often the same parallel can be drawn between mothers and daughters. The mother portrays herself, consciously or unconsciously, as being perfect. This occurs quite naturally. After all, a daughter can easily put on a pedestal the woman who has fed and cared for her from birth. The result? Her standard is unattainable—impossible to live up to. The daughter compares herself to her mother and consistently comes up short.

The daughter of a perfect mother, a mannequin, finds this very painful. She feels the same kind of hurt that comes when you visualize yourself wearing the dress that looks perfect on the mannequin, but discover that it doesn't fit when you try it on.

I have a friend who has a problem with being self-critical. Her attitude stems from a huge dose of insecurity.

So, I thought, *I wonder what her relationship is with her mother.* On one occasion I asked her. She said, "My mother was killed when I was four." "What was she like?" I queried. "My mother loved being a homemaker. In fact, some people I know said she was the best cook in the county." Her eyes lit up with pride as she continued. "Others said she was the kindest woman who ever lived." She continued to speak of her mom in glowing tones.

Suddenly everything fell into place. I realized that my friend had unconsciously adopted a mannequin as a model: she saw her mother as the perfect model, without blemish. Her model is not a living, breathing woman. Hers is an image, an impression of what her mother was according to the descriptions and stories she received from her father and brother and neighbors.

It's pretty difficult to live up to a perfect model and to compare yourself to a flawless standard. Clearly she faces difficulties in living up to the image of an incomparable woman, an image she has carried with her all these years. Her beliefs concerning her mother created the problem.

Mannequins, Models, and Mothers

The idea of perfection that originated in my friend's young mind and which later served to inspire her to become all she could be was never intended to be a damaging psychological force in her life. But it was. The results were unintentional, but destructive.

The mannequin without flaws cannot do the job of modeling as well as the woman who stumbles now and then. Why? The mannequin is dead—lifeless. However even the most inept *live* models have the possibility of improvement and can offer hope, because they are just that—alive!

Unfortunately, some mothers intentionally play the role of a mannequin. Afraid to show their shortcomings, they put on a deliberate false front. I use the word *deliberate* because much of this charade is a self-protective mechanism. The mother uses this technique to avoid facing her weaknesses and areas of need in her own life. In so doing she does a horrible injustice to her daughters. It's impossible for a daughter to compare favorably with this kind of model. The result? Many daughters suffer needless trauma. They become insecure and critical of themselves and others. If only mothers would realize that daughters need real mothers—*living* models with whom they can identify, not *perfect* ones! Surely the ideal model is one who can exhibit her strengths without hiding her weaknesses. Every mother can be an ideal model.

The Stumblers

What about the second group of models? While sitting at Bullocks, watching the various women pass between the tables, we see one kind who form a small group of elite women, those who stand out as the stars of the show. We'll discuss them later. Then there are the others: Let's call them the stumblers. This group includes the young and inexperienced apprentices and the older, more experienced models who still lack that special quality that makes a star.

Many mothers fit into this less-than-the-best category.

I visited a friend of mine recently and asked her about her relationship with her mother. She seemed very positive about it, except in one area. She complained she could not talk to her mother about her marriage. "I can share openly with her on any subject," my friend said, "except about my relationship with my husband. I don't know why." Then she looked at me, the light suddenly dawning. "Perhaps it's because her own life was a failure in that area. I mean—daddy left mom last year, for another woman. I guess I'm afraid to follow her advice, for fear that my marriage would fail, too."

My friend took an important step when she finally recognized her reasons for closing off part of her life from her mother. I hope she will not stop there, but will look carefully at her mother's role as a wife, identify her mistakes, and learn from them.

Mothers are human, and all make mistakes. No one escapes. Ask most mothers—mine included—"When was the last time you really blew it?" They would probably say, "How about yesterday?" Understandably when a mother trips and falls flat on her face, especially when the fall is painful, daughters fear following the trail that leads to such hurt.

The models who have had a bad day are understandably embarrassed and distressed by their failure. Stumbling while you model a beautiful evening gown makes anyone want to leave town on the next fast train. But mothers can't leave town. Nor can they lie there with their faces on the ground. They have to pick themselves up because they have families to take care of. Mothers must not keep punishing themselves for failing. They must not indulge in self-flagellation and self-pity and other such painful and unnecessary reactions!

Like the stumbling model, a mother must stand up, hold her head up high and try again. She must take that first painful step down the ramp again. This time she checks the length of the gown more carefully and double-checks the heels of the shoes to see that they won't cause her to fall. The ramp must be examined for loose carpeting that could cause a further embarrassing situation.

The model who really wants to be a star learns to pick herself up, to avoid pitfalls the next time around, and to keep on trying. So it is with mothers. My mom was great on reaching beyond her failures. Often I'd hear her say, "I'm sorry."

Mothers need to dry their tears and find consolation in the fact that they are not the only ones who have tripped. Every mother has had days she wishes she could wipe out forever. I'm not the only young mother who has taken the phone off the hook, drawn the drapes, locked the doors, and despairingly cried for hours.

When you trip, it's a great opportunity, if someone's around to pick up the pieces, to help to "put mommy together again." Often daughters are the perfect choice for this delicate operation. They can be a remarkable source of courage in renewing a mother's confidence.

Most mothers, like the models we've seen, fit into this second, rather broad category. Yet all of them have the potential to become stars, and some of them will even become showstoppers. How can a mother do this?

The Queens

Every fashion show includes at least one showstopper—the model with regal bearing. When she gracefully glides down the ramp and aisles, everyone sees a successful woman whose movements are under control. She commands her audience, and they love it. Everyone feels comfortable watching her. The clothes look right on her; they fit nicely, not too loose and not too tight. The color compliments her complexion, and the style suits her personality. She knows what is right for her.

She seems nearly perfect. But she did not always look so. It took years of experience and practice. Like every other model, she had to take that first step down the ramp. Her nerves fluttered wildly before every show, and her movements and turns were unpolished and slightly awkward. In some humiliating moments, she, too, stumbled, and her lack of expertise readily showed.

But this model didn't surrender to her embarrassing times. Instead she decided to learn from them, to persevere and improve her skills. Today we see the results. She may not look absolutely perfect; she still seeks excellence, her best. Her appearance is fresh and lovely; not stilted and posed, but real and genuine.

Every mother holds the potential to become such a regal, graceful model for her daughter. Let me emphasize: This woman is not perfect, not without flaws. Still vulnerable, but striving for excellence, she does her best. Each mother, like the models, chooses to exhibit a different style.

Show-stopping models show different strengths and talents, but they've made the best of their abilities. Mothers are the same. They differ in the gifts and opportunities that are given to them. What they do with them and what they become separates the stars from the ordinary models.

My mother, for example, is a star. Although she might be considered inferior to other women in some areas, she has learned how to turn her weaknesses into strengths. That's why, in my opinion, she falls into the star category. She is successful enough to become my ideal. She stumbled, but she learned. Her mistakes never got the best of her; rather she has gotten the best of them.

I vividly recall a day when I came bursting through the door. "Mom, wait till you hear! Why, I couldn't believe my eyes!" I proceeded to describe my juicy bit of gossip, in every gory detail, as high-school students can do so well.

"Sheila, sit down a minute. I have a story I think you need to hear." She paused and hesitated. I could tell that what she had to say was difficult for her. "I was only a young pastor's wife, lonely, far from home and family. Dad and I were just married and had taken our first church. In my need to make new friends, I found someone in the church with whom I began to spend time. Unfortunately, one day I found myself confiding something that your father shared with me. It was about someone in the church, who had come to see him privately. I had no business breaking his confidence by sharing it with my friend. But I did.

"To my utter embarrassment, this same church member who had seen your father, approached me when there was no one else around. 'Arvella,' she said, 'I was very disturbed to hear that you repeated something to your friend, something I told your husband in confidence. Now it's all over town. Fortunately, it was not any news that will destroy me, but this gossiping of yours will destroy you and your husband's ministry. You are young. I urge you to never again betray your husband's confidence.'"

Mom flushed as she recounted the tale. But she continued, "Sheila, I learned from my mistake. I never again told something to someone when I was asked to keep it private. I just hope that you will learn from my blunder and that you can be spared the same embarrassment."

She picked herself up when she fell, brushed herself

off, and emerged from this experience a much wiser and more gracious woman. She had betrayed a confidence, but determined that it would never happen again. In sharing this experience with me, she modeled reality. She effectively influenced my life.

Mothers must lead and model, and daughters should learn and follow. Sometimes the most successful moms will also learn and become better persons by observing their daughters' lives. Let's look at these two propositions. Ordinarily daughters are not called to be judges or critics of their mothers' modeling. Rather they should observe. However there are instances in which a daughter must critically evaluate her mother's performance because of the extremely poor modeling job her mother provides. Lives have been saved, families spared disaster because a courageous daughter has had enough spunk to choose another way. Normally, however, daughters should be learning life qualities and character traits from their mothers. Once I was not so generous in my affections for mom. I did not always eagerly follow in her footsteps. I mistook her leads as orders and her guidelines as restrictions.

I was only twelve, but I was really bugged. *Who does she think she is, anyway?* I declared to myself, in the privacy of my room. *She's always telling me what to do. She makes me work so hard. If it's not the dishes, then it's the laundry. And once the laundry's done, then it's the bathrooms. Man, Cinderella was living on easy street compared with me.*

Mom's requests certainly weren't out of line, but

my budding sense of independence rebelled at her demands. I found my resentments piling up until there was a wall the size of China's separating us. Fortunately, I encountered a very wise counselor at camp that summer. I feared telling anyone about my trouble with my mother, but I really hurt. I wanted to make things right.

After I hesitantly shared the negative feelings I had been harboring for mother, my counselor replied, "You know, Sheila, mothers need love, too. She gives and gives and gives for you every day. It's scary being a mother. It's the biggest responsibility in the world. The only way mothers know whether or not they're doing a good job is through us—their daughters. We're the only assurance they can have that they're doing okay.

"When was the last time you told her you loved her?"

To my embarrassment, I couldn't remember.

My counselor continued. "When you get home, give your mother a big hug and tell her that you love her. Do it again the next day and the next, for one whole week. Then write me and let me know how it's going."

I arrived home from camp, filled with apprehension. I wanted to try what my counselor had suggested, but I wasn't sure I could bring myself to do it. The hours stretched by as I watched mom move around the house. Every time I had worked up the nerve to go over and hug her, I'd chicken out. Fear, anxiety, and a multitude of emotions kept me from going to her in love.

Mannequins, Models, and Mothers 25

Finally, as night approached, I watched mom prepare our evening meal. Her shoulders were bowed with fatigue. I heard my younger brother and sister, fighting. The phone rang with calls from women who needed prayer and counseling.

Suddenly I realized how much she did for me, Bob, and Jeanne, and for the ladies at church. It dawned on me how much she needed my help. Why, her requests weren't demands—they were pleas for help!

"Mom," I said softly. "I love you."

She looked up, surprised. I hesitantly put my arms around her neck and hugged her. It felt good! We smiled at each other, through our tears, and experienced the love that is uniquely shared between a mother and daughter.

To this day, when my mother seems upset and out of sorts, I stop and remember my counselor's words, "Moms need love, too." Then I'll give mom a hug and whisper again how much I love her. It's amazing how a little love cleared up my perspective.

Such resentment is a common issue between mothers and daughters.

A few years ago, when working at the church as a counselor for the junior-high, senior-high and college-age girls, I repeatedly heard stories from daughters who were feeling resentment toward their mothers. The majority of them had simply lost perspective. They had gotten hung up on their mothers' authority and directions and couldn't see the beauty and order that their mothers were trying to bring to their lives.

So I prescribed the same exercise that had worked

for me: "Hug your mother and tell her that you love her every day for a week."

I was amazed at the results. Girl after girl reported the following, "My mother and I get along so well now. She's just like a close girl friend. She's not like a mother at all."

Was it the mother who changed, or the daughter? Both changed. The mother felt needed, loved, successful. The daughter looked beyond herself and saw her mother for what she really was: a human being striving and longing to be a successful mother.

There's a star inside all mothers. The unfortunate mothers who, like mannequins, insist on maintaining the myth of their perfection, and by so doing live in an unreal world, will never break through into reality. They will stay as lifeless models. Only when they are willing to strip away this false image can they, too, have the potential to become queens.

Part I

Between Mother and Daughter—
Modeling

2

Free to Be—You and Me

At a typical fashion show, in the course of an afternoon, each model displays a variety of clothes. She wears something sporty at the beginning of the show and dashes backstage to change into a glamorous evening gown. Then she sheds the gown to don a slinky negligee and finally winds up her part of the show with a grand-finale mink stole. Another model wears a classic blazer, and no show is complete without a display of the latest accessories. As I watch fashion shows, several outfits appeal to me. Some catch my eye because they are beautiful, pleasing to the eye. Others demand my attention because I realize that particular style would flatter my build. Other considerations include the color, the price, and adaptability to my present wardrobe.

In the same way, mothers model a variety of values and beliefs for daughters. Perhaps you are the athletic type: You exhibit the importance of physical fitness. Or maybe you like elegance: You probably demonstrate the importance of grace and beauty. Perhaps your tastes are traditional: You love tried and true ginghams and display warmth and stability. On the other hand, you may enjoy the contemporary: Clean, uncluttered, lines and novel color combinations excite you; you model the importance of moving ahead and the fulfillment of being a pacesetter. Finally, you may be the frilly, bows, lace, and eyelet type: You display the sheer loveliness of femininity.

More than likely you are a unique mixture of the above ingredients. Our differences make each of us beautiful in our own way. Together we complete the stunning picture of womanhood. The different colors and hues give the picture its depth. What a boring picture would result from the artist's using only one color. God made each mother and daughter individual, so that each contributes her unique beauty to the world.

Daughters are individuals, too. I must give my children the freedom to be themselves. They need to go their own way and become the persons they were meant to be; I am only a model. That's what mothers should be. My mother displays the values she believes in, but cannot force me to accept them. Only I can choose whether or not to don them. Many mothers experience difficulty in giving their daughters this freedom to choose. The bonds of love cling so strongly, so tightly, and the mother-hen syndrome is powerful.

Look what happens in the beginning.

Bonding

Throughout nature, the attachment of a mother to her young is evident. We see it in the kangaroo and the opossum, who carry their babies with them wherever they go. These animals, among a zoo of others, exhibit the continuing attachment of mother and baby. After birth, a newborn depends on his mother as much as he did in the womb, perhaps even more so. In the womb, the mother entirely provides the fetus's food, oxygen, and protection. After birth, with the exception of oxygen, the child still depends on his mother for survival, only now he also fights for emotional survival.

Babies are thinking, feeling, emotional beings at birth. Studies have shown that babies require love, caresses, and strokes from their mothers in order to live. Those denied all affection cannot survive for more than three months. Consequently pediatricians now stress *bonding:* the emotional attachment between mother and infant. Bonding—or emotional food—is as vital to a child as is his physical nourishment.

Letting Go

Although mothers and their young naturally form deep attachments, at some point nature also urges us to let our children go. The fine-line tension between bonding and letting go is one of the most difficult aspects of motherhood. As cruel as it may seem, the mother wolf abandons her cub; the mother bird pushes her babies from the nest. But her actions are not really heartless; they are essential. In fact it is just as vital for us to let our children go as it is for us to form emotional attachments to them.

Inevitably the time comes when daughters cease to be little girls. They grow into young women and learn to function as adults. My mother always strongly supported this concept. My brother and sisters and I always knew that we were expected to go away to college upon high-school graduation. Although I expected the day when I would have to leave home and be nudged from the nest, I still found it difficult when it actually came.

As a high-school student, I was typically preoccupied with a myriad of interests: boys, extracurricular activities, school plays, and concert choir performances. My list of priorities did not include my relationship with my mother. We loved each other, enjoyed each other, and got along fine. But it took leaving home for four years to show me *how* much I loved and admired her and how important her input continued to be.

I felt frightened as I stepped off the plane in Holland, Michigan. Three thousand miles away from everyone I knew and loved, in this tiny midwestern town, I was a total stranger. I knew absolutely no one. It didn't take long to make acquaintances, but it took years to find friends. Some girls I spent time with, whom I thought cared about me, really didn't care. I spent most of my freshman year looking for a true friend.

In the meantime, I observed all the girls I lived with. They were all so different, especially in their values and beliefs. I found myself in many rap sessions, examining and defending the values I had been taught from birth. I could no longer take for granted the lessons I learned at my mother's knee. I realized that mom's beliefs could not be mine simply through

Free to Be—You and Me

osmosis. I needed to take my own stand. Often I unconsciously went through the process of evaluating my parents' value system.

As I talked with my classmates for hours, many of them challenged the beliefs I had been taught. What thrilled me was that my mother constantly came out on top. Her values withstood the test of the highest philosophical order: the test of collegiate interrogation. I gave mom and her values an A and decided to adopt them for myself.

For example I realized that the Ten Commandments were not merely a list of rules and regulations, but rather a list of guidelines that could lead me to the happiest life possible. So I chose to believe in one God—the loving, all-powerful God described in the New Testament. I chose to believe in His Son, Jesus, and in His death and resurrection: historical, life-changing events that occurred *for her and for me!* I chose to make the Ten Commandments a foundation for my life. On reflection I became aware that mother had built her life on this same rock, and I followed her example. But as much as I wanted to be like mother, I also needed to be me.

Setting a child free to "become" is essential for parents and children. Stilted, deformed people can be the unhappy result of a mother's failure to let go.

Mother-daughter relationships change. Dependent little girls should develop into independent, grown women. The release usually occurs over a period of time. To be successful, it must be accompanied by parental permission for the daughter to choose and backed by unconditional support, no matter the consequences of the choice.

A true story in *Guideposts* magazine told about a young girl who went through a crisis experience. The mother and daughter faced a terribly difficult time. The daughter, whom I shall call Sally, began dating a guy who looked like nothing but trouble. The mother fought the relationship with everything she could. She started by reasoning with Sally, eventually pleaded with her, and finally absolutely forbade her to see him.

As Sally's mother fought her daughter's relationship with the boyfriend, her relationship with Sally began to deteriorate. Sally no longer spoke to her mother when she came home. More and more she withdrew to her bedroom. When her mother confronted Sally, she met with more and more defiance, until one night Sally announced, "Mother, in three weeks I will be eighteen. Nothing you or daddy can do can stop me. Bill and I are going to California to live with his sister."

Her mother watched her one and only daughter, her baby girl, coldly turn her back on her and walk away. Frantic and tormented, she began to pray, "Please, Lord, show me what to do."

She turned to the story of the Prodigal Son, in her Bible. She read Jesus' words as He shared about a father's love: a love that is willing to let go and welcome home again, no matter what mistakes are made.

This brave mother knew what she should do. She gently knocked on Sally's door. "Yeah?" was Sally's reply.

"Sally, can I come in for a minute? I want to talk to you."

"Sure. But nothing you say can make me stay."

"I know that," she said as she sat on the bed by her daughter. "Sally, if you want to go, neither your father nor I will stand in your way. We would much rather have you stay here with us, but we can't force you to. You are an adult now, and you must make your own decisions. However, I do want you to know that if you should change your mind, you will always be welcome back."

Sally looked at her mother. She was puzzled, surprised, but convinced that her mother was sincere. As the weeks went by, Sally never said a word to her mother. On the morning of her eighteenth birthday, she came out of her room, suitcase in hand. Meekly she said, "Well—I'm going now."

Her mother choked back the panic that rushed through her, resisting the urge to throw her arms around her daughter and cry, "Don't go! Please don't go!" Instead, she calmly replied, "Oh, Sally. I will miss you. Please, understand this: I love you. I will always be here for you."

For this mother, the day was filled with torment as well as prayers for her daughter. That night the phone rang. "Mom, this is Sally." Her voice broke, and she cried, "I want to come home! Bill doesn't love me. He's not the kind of man I want. Please, can I come home?"

What a powerful example of a mother unconditionally freeing her daughter to become. This story turned out well, but let's face it: It doesn't always work out that way. That's part of the risk. Such releasing may result in much pain for mother.

Facing Disappointment

When she was young, my mother dreamed of becoming a concert organist. She first fell in love with the great instrument in her small hometown in Iowa. Little Newkirk consists of a church on one corner, a school on another, a general store on the third, and a cornfield on the fourth. In that country church mom reveled in the music of Bach as she practiced for hours.

Her love for music brought her to a new love: her husband. Dad met mom one Sunday afternoon as he sought out the organist of Newkirk Reformed Church, where he was scheduled to preach. Dad immediately recognized her as the girl for him. He fell head over heels in love, and one year later they were married, in that same little church.

Although mom kept busy playing the organ for dad's new church in California, her hectic schedule left very little time for practice. As more and more children came upon the scene, she knew she would never fulfill her dream.

Consequently, when I showed a flair for music and a love for the piano, mom hoped that someday I would be the organist she had never been able to be.

"Sheila, I'm going to take you to hear some of the most beautiful music you've ever heard," she announced one night. At eight years old, I wasn't too impressed. "Where are we going?" I asked unenthusiastically.

"A concert! An organ concert! It is going to be held

Free to Be—You and Me

in a beautiful old church in Los Angeles! You're going to love it!"

I wasn't too sure. "Flipper" sounded much more exciting than listening to someone play an organ all night.

But off we went. I sat behind a huge old pillar in a stuffy old church. I couldn't see a thing except for that big, old pillar! And the music was boring! All I wanted to do was go to sleep. I longed to go home and go to bed, and I vowed that I would never again allow my mother to take me to another "one of these things!"

I wasn't old enough or sensitive enough to see the tears in my mother's eyes. For her, the concert unleashed all her unfulfilled dreams. The concert held hope for her. Through it perhaps I, her daughter, would fulfill her dreams.

Mom exclaimed after it was over, "My! Wasn't that gorgeous? Do you think you'd like to learn to play the organ someday, Sheila?"

Not realizing how important this was to her, I replied bluntly. "No! It's a boring old instrument!"

What bitter disappointment she must have suffered. Her dream was now twice dashed to the ground. Yet she managed to hide her feelings, allowing me the freedom to choose my own instrument. I regret that hurt mom has felt over the years, but never did I feel guilty for not choosing the organ. The instrument was hers, not mine. She realized it, and never again pushed it on me. The choice was mine, not hers. She set me free to become the woman I was meant to be.

3

Responsibility or Response-Ability

To love our children and still be willing to let them go is an excellent goal. Accomplishing that goal is a lifetime work for many mothers. I'm sure it will be for me. With just two years of marriage and one new baby boy, I'm increasingly aware of how hard it is to "let go." I feel so *responsible:* not just for Jason, but for my husband, Jim—everyone and everything I touch in my role as wife and mother.

Not long ago I grasped a warm mug of coffee in my hands and sat back contentedly. "Ah!" I sighed, "Jason's asleep, the washing machine is going, the dishes are done, the bed is made. Now it's time to just relax."

I no sooner put my head back than I heard the whir of the automatic garage door. *That's strange,* I thought. *Who could that be?*

My husband wearily walked through the door. His pale, drawn face worried me, not to mention the fact that it was only ten o'clock in the morning.

"Jim," I said. "What's wrong?"

"I'm sick. I think I've got a fever." He headed for our upstairs bedroom.

Responsibility or Response-Ability

"I could make up the sofa for you," I called after him.

"No, thank you. I'm afraid I'm too sick for that." I groaned. When Jim had pleaded with me for a new two-story home, I had agreed on one condition: when he was sick, he'd stay downstairs.

Obviously he had forgotten our agreement, and I could tell this was not the time to remind him. So:

"Sheila, would you bring me some more water?"

"Sure, honey. Coming."

"Sheila, I'm cold. Do we have any more blankets?"

"Coming, honey."

"Isn't it time for my next pill?"

"Coming, honey."

My legs felt increasingly heavy. Each step felt like a mini mountain. Finally Jim fell asleep. *Maybe I could heat up that cup of coffee,* I thought. But before I could take so much as one sip, I heard from the nursery, "Wah! Wah!" Jason's cries pierced through the house and grated on my frazzled nerves. I gulped, mustered all the love I could, and bounded up the stairs for the umpteenth time that day.

"Coming, Jason."

I picked up my screaming baby. He was burning up!

"Oh, no. Not Jason, too!" Sure enough, he had a fever.

Often during the week that followed, I'd feel a feverish chill sweep through me as I diligently nursed my "boys." Remarkably, I was able to keep going.

You can't get sick, Sheila, I'd tell myself. *Someone*

has to take care of Jim and Jason. And so, through sheer willpower, I kept going.

Where did that willpower come from? It came from the knowledge that I, and I alone, was responsible. I often wondered where my mother had gotten her energy to care for us when we were sick or to sit up through the night, typing last-minute term papers. Now I know where her extra reserve of energy came from: the deep sense of responsibility, the knowledge that no one else could do it for her. When I became aware that I *alone* held the responsibility for Jim's and Jason's care, then I was forced to tap a reserve well of energy.

Accepting Responsibility

Responsibility is as synonymous with *motherhood* as *love*. Every mother feels overwhelmed by it the moment she brings her tiny infant home from the hospital. That first moment when you are alone in your home, holding your helpless baby—no nurses to summon, no mother to call—can be frightening. Not only do you have the responsibility of changing your baby's diapers, feeding him, of loving him, you stand responsible for his very *life!*

Every day I sat and cradled my boy to my bosom, looking at his gentle, trusting eyes. Wonder filled me when I thought: *I—Sheila—am responsible for Jason's life!* Some days I felt overjoyed, so proud that God entrusted me with such a beautiful little life. But other days I crumbled into tears of dismay; surely I did everything wrong!

Responsibility or Response-Ability 41

Responsibility, will it make me or break me? Will I be challenged, motivated, uplifted? Or will I be buried by its overwhelming weight? Will I be paralyzed by the very natural fears and apprehensions that come with this new role? My own mother has done much to help me balance my sense of responsibility with my fears of "what might happen" to my family.

Until recently I didn't know my mother once lived in fear that something might happen to one of us. She feared we would be hit by a car, fall out of a tree, or become deathly ill. When I first experienced the overwhelming sense of responsibility for Jason, I called mom and said, "I don't know if I can take it! I am so afraid of being a horrible mother. What if I say or do something that emotionally scars Jason for the rest of his life? What if I don't watch him carefully enough, and he has an accident? What if I'm not feeding him the right kinds of foods? And what if . . . ?"

Mom suddenly interrupted me. "Sheila, you can't live in the fear of 'what if . . . ?' It will destroy you. You'll become so paralyzed that neither you nor Jason will find the joy in life God intends you to have. I know how you feel. For years I felt the same way about you and your brother and sisters. Finally I realized that I was doing a disservice to you and to myself, not to mention my faith in God.

"Turn Jason over to God. After all, God loves him even more than you do. God knew that you, with all your strengths and weaknesses, were the ideal mother for Jason. Give Jason to God, and He will fill in all the gaps. Where your love is too protective and too weak, there God will be, smoothing out your efforts, helping Jason become all He wants him to be."

Through talks like that I've realized the freedom that comes with entrusting your children to God. And in so doing I've discovered that my responsibilities can be enjoyed, not just endured.

The answer lies in the word itself. For if you look at it carefully, responsibility is merely *response-ability*, the ability to respond to my child's needs. If, as a mother, I accept that task, I am being responsible. Beyond that I must turn the outcome of any circumstance or situation over to God.

Let Go and Let God

Last Christmas I got a taste of just what "letting go and letting God" means. That December all the baby magazines warned that accidents were more likely to happen the closer to Christmas it got and the busier we mothers became. *That's excellent advice!* I agreed and vowed I would be extra careful with Jason. On Christmas Eve, however, my active six-month-old was getting underfoot. He was gleefully unwrapping presents as soon as I finished them. His little walker scooted across the kitchen, and he grabbed a handful of Christmas bread dough, rising on the open oven door. Flour, wrappings, raisins, and bread dough scattered everywhere. But I had never been happier. I sang the Christmas carols as high as my voice would go, and Jason laughed delightedly. Finally, with my last batch of bread in the oven, I decided to retreat to

Responsibility or Response-Ability 43

our sunny California patio to finish embroidering mom's towels, her Christmas present.

I quickly placed Jason on the patio, in his walker, while I dashed inside for a chair and my embroidery. I was gone only two minutes. But before I reached the door I heard a shrill cry. *Where is he?* I thought. *What's happened?*

Then I remembered: There was a three-inch drop on one side of our patio, where we hadn't finished our landscaping. Sure enough, there was Jason—facedown in his walker, his screams muffled by the pieces of broken cement. I frantically picked him up, gasping, "Oh, Jason! I'm so sorry!" The mud and dirt that covered him hid his hurts, but I could see traces of blood beginning to seep through. We cried together, until finally Jason looked up at me curiously. He realized I was crying with him, so he stopped. Then through the mud and the blood and the tears, he smiled. What relief I felt.

"He's all right!" Sure enough, after cleaning off the dirt, I could see only two little nicks. Jason was okay. Both of us had merely had a good scare. I had never before been so frightened.

Although Jason appeared unhurt, that day I continued to carry a tremendous burden of guilt. I was depressed, convinced I was a horrible mother—negligent. Add any other negative adjective, and it described how I felt.

Under this heavy cloud, that night I attended our church's Christmas Eve candlelight service. Looking back, I realize I hadn't been negligent. In fact, I'd been very careful with Jason, in spite of the hurried preparations for the day. But as I sat down in the pew I felt wretched. I sent up a prayer asking for forgiveness, though I really didn't know why I sought it.

Throughout the service I saw Jason facedown in the rocks. I imagined his eyes wide with terror as he fell. I heard his cries over and over again. All the while I continued to pray. "Please, dear Lord. Help me forgive myself for being so irresponsible."

As the service drew to an end, I still did not feel the peace or forgiveness I had prayed for. But as hundreds of people flocked to the altar steps, for a Christmas prayer, I found myself desperately joining them. As I knelt on the gleaming marble, the candles shimmering all around me, I closed my eyes again to pray that I would feel the peace and joy of Christmas. Once again I envisioned little Jason, facedown on the cement, but suddenly I saw two large hands reach out and cushion my baby's face. Jason was caught by God's gentle hands. At that moment God dramatically showed me what my mother had been sharing with me all along: When we turn our children over to Him, He protects them. That night I realized the truth of mom's words, "God loves our children more than we do. They have only been loaned to us. In the final analysis, they belong to Him."

These are not merely empty words; mom has lived them. In the summer of 1978, I drove my parents and my sisters to the Los Angeles airport. Carol and Gretchen were about to take off for my aunt and uncle's

Responsibility or Response-Ability

farm, in Iowa. Jeanne was leaving for a summer semester in Israel, and mom and dad were destined for a conference in Korea. The three flights were scheduled on three different airlines, with departure times one hour apart.

I pulled up to the Western terminal, where mom and dad quickly unloaded Carol and Gretchen's bags. They whisked them up to their flight. When mom met us at Jeanne's terminal, she haltingly shared how she accompanied thirteen-year-old Carol and eleven-year-old Gretchen to their seats. "Carol clutched the stuffed dog dad bought for her, and Gretchen hugged her doll. They looked so young to be flying all the way to Iowa by themselves. I guess Carol felt my apprehension, for she suddenly looked as mature as a thirteen-year-old could and said, 'Mom, don't worry about us. We'll be fine. I'll take real good care of Gretchen.' "

Mom looked as if she was about to cry, but we were all drawn back to reality as we heard the call for Jeanne's flight. Jeanne was off; and one hour later, I waved my final good-bye to mom and dad.

The weeks flew by. Before I knew it, it was the night before I was to return to Los Angeles International Airport to pick up Carol and Gretchen. I was looking forward to seeing them, for I had missed them. As I returned from a date with my fiancé, I shared my excitement at the prospect of seeing my sisters.

I no sooner stepped inside my apartment than the phone rang. Since it was late, I was surprised and anxious to hear my father's associate on the other end.

"Sheila, there has been an accident. Carol's been hurt."

So I learned that my sister was lying in the hospital, undergoing emergency amputation of her left leg. Apparently she had begged our cousin, Mark, to take her riding on his motorcycle, as a last fling before they were to leave the Iowa farm. Mark eventually gave in to Carol's pleas and took Carol on that fateful ride. But thanks to his insistence, it was not a *fatal* ride. For the helmet Mark insisted she wear saved her life that night on the Iowa gravel road when he swerved to avoid driving into the rear end of the car that had suddenly stopped immediately in front of them. In swerving to the left of that vehicle, Mark drove head-on into the path of another car that suddenly loomed out of the darkness. Carol's leg bore the brunt of the collision, and she was hurled through the air, landing in a ditch. She lost thirteen units of blood before they could get her to the hospital.

On hearing this news, I felt stunned. As difficult as this was for me to take, I had to pull myself together. Someone had to call mom and dad in Korea and break the news to them. It had to be me.

I prayed for strength as I gave the numbers to the overseas operator. I heard the phone ring.

"Hello?" It was my father.

"Dad, this is Sheila. I have bad news. . . . Carol's been in an accident." Mom came on the line. Although she was thousands of miles away, I felt as though we were in the same room.

"Her leg was smashed beyond repair," I continued. "They—they're amputating it now."

Responsibility or Response-Ability

I will never forget her response. An agonizing silence followed, then tears. Finally in a whisper she repeated ever so slowly: "All—things—work—together—for—good—to—them—that—love—the—Lord.

"Sheila. Your father and I will take the first flight we can get and fly straight to Iowa. That takes almost a day in itself, however. So will you go to Iowa immediately and stay with Carol until we can get there?"

I assured her that I would.

After she hung up, mom turned to dad and told him of my call. They clung to each other and let the tears flow freely. Half a world away, there was nothing they could do for their daughter in her greatest time of need—nothing except to pray. Mom clung to dad, and they prayed, "Dear God, thank You that You love Carol more than we do! Guide the hands of the surgeon now. Jesus, You are the healing Physician. Surround Carol now with Your holy and healing presence."

In that moment they relinquished their daughter to God, Carol's Creator. And in that act of relinquishment, they found strength. Their belief in an all-powerful God—a Heavenly Father—held mom together during their long flight home. That night she wrote in her diary:

> The night seems dark and long. In reality, it is a short night, for we are traveling east, and only six hours from now the dawn will break. There is little or no talking, just a feeling of "being one," be-

tween Bob and me as we go through our first tragedy together.

There is no sleep. I close my eyes. but over and over again, all I can see is Carol in terrible pain. If only I could have been with her. There are no thoughts of guilt, and I am surprised. Often I had feelings of guilt as I left the children for a trip with my husband. Whether it was for work or rest, I knew the children were in good hands, and I would decide to be with my husband. How often I thought—and the thought would be a prayer—*Jesus, keep them safe.* Now it has happened. . . .

I am on a trip, and there is an accident. How I want to be there. "Oh, Carol, how did you stand the pain?"

The tears flow fast and often, and the Kleenex pile up. The stewardess quietly and gently gathers them as she walks up and down the aisle.

It is light enough to read now without disturbing the other passengers, so I reach into my flight bag for the Bible I packed and turn to the *Living Psalms.* My eyes search for comfort and fall to the last portion of Psalms 57, verse 7: "O God, my heart is quiet and confident." Yes, there is not the faintest twinge of guilt. Bob and I are confident that Carol is in God's hands.

Indeed, mom had nothing to fear. Carol was in good hands. The thigh was mutilated beyond recognition. Miraculously, however, the surgeon decided not to remove it.

When mom and dad finally arrived at Saint Joseph's Hospital in Sioux City, Iowa, nearly thirty-three hours later, Carol greeted them with a smile that illuminated

Responsibility or Response-Ability

her sterile intensive-care room. "Oh, mom!" she cried out painfully. "Oh, dad! I'm so glad to see you! Please, don't feel bad. I'm going to be okay. You see, I know God has allowed this to happen. I think He wants to use me to help others who are hurting."

Mom had prayerfully turned Carol over to God, in her hotel room in Korea. Half a world away, He answered her prayer. It was obvious to all of us that God had enveloped Carol and had comforted her when we couldn't.

Today, Carol has turned her scar into a star. She grew into a beautiful young woman, both inside and out. Although she and mom spent countless hours in therapy and prosthesis fittings, her life is full. You could hardly call her a handicapped person. She is far more active and she has accomplished more in athletics than I ever will!

As I write these words, the pangs of pain and sorrow experienced at the time of Carol's accident want to erupt again. The fortitude and faith expressed by mother on that occasion left an indelible imprint on my life. I would gladly follow her modeling in any other crisis that may come my way. The lesson is clear: Relying on God's strength, I must respond to life's situations with all the abilities He has given. In so doing I learn how to be a responsible mother. But more is required of me: It is only in the yielding of the final outcome to God that a mother finds herself adequate for her God-given task.

4

Accept, Accept, Accept

Accept is mom's favorite word. It pops up in many of our conversations. Whatever the problem, whenever she's called on for advice, she inevitably says, "Accept it." She believes freedom comes with acceptance, that there is power in acceptance. Frankly I agree. Whenever I stop fighting the negatives in every situation and in every person, then I am free to see and appreciate their positive aspects.

Seeing the positive side of my singleness seemed impossible. Singleness appeared to be a burden I had to bear; and the longer I bore it, the heavier it got. I thought my singleness caused my unhappiness, and the solution to my depression and despondency was obvious: marriage. But year after year went by, and the possibility of marriage seemed to get farther and farther away. My happiness appeared to be an elusive, hopeless dream.

In my loneliest times, I talked to my folks and said, "What's wrong with me? Why can't I find a man who wants to marry me? If only I had a husband who loved me as much as dad loves you, mother, then I'd never again feel lonely or depressed!"

"Don't you know a man can't make you happy? The

Accept, Accept, Accept

only person who can do that is you! You've got to *accept* your singleness. God has allowed you to be single at this time in your life for a very important reason. Although you may not understand His plan, you must accept the fact that His timing is always perfect and best. If you continue to fight it, you will destroy yourself. But if you can accept you singleness and can enjoy the freedom of a single's schedule, *then* you'll be happy, and *only* then! You don't want to depend on someone else for your happiness. Why, there is no man on earth who can make you happy all the time. People are human and imperfect, and there will be times when we can't meet all of our loved ones' needs. We can only love them, believe in them, and help them to see the beauty that's in their lives right now!"

The importance of this counsel didn't sink in overnight. But finally God gave me the ability to accept my singleness. What a great day that was! Suddenly it dawned on me: I had a lot to offer other people.

Eventually I accepted my one-bedroom apartment and actually learned to enjoy moments of solitude in the midst of a busy schedule.

I found myself thanking God that I didn't have to rush home at 4:30 to prepare a meal for someone, but I could instead stay and work until 6:00 or 7:00 or even 8:00, if I felt really inspired. When at the last minute, mom and dad invited me to accompany them on a trip, I was glad I could get away at such short notice and take advantage of my freedom.

Don't misunderstand. I still desired the in-depth relationship with a man that only comes with the commitment of marriage. My acceptance of living alone had to be a daily experience. But through this acceptance, I found the freedom to live those single days to their fullest. Now I look back on them fondly. I rejoice that I had as many as I did. Ultimately, it was the trials I encountered, the lessons I learned, and the experiences to which I was exposed, that prepared me for an exciting marriage.

Learning Acceptance

Well, eventually my long-dreamed-of day came: I became a wife. It was great! But I quickly discovered that married life had its ups and downs. My Prince Charming was not a make-believe character out of a fairy tale; he was human. The iron will I had admired so much before marriage suddenly appeared to me as sheer stubbornness.

I remember putting through a call to my mother. It went something like this: "How can *anyone* be so stubborn? How can he possibly expect me to do this? Why do *I* always have to bend and be accommodating?"

You probably know the answer before I tell you. "Accept him, Sheila! He's not perfect, but he is a wonderful man! I don't think you could find anyone better than Jim. Sure, he may be as stubborn as you say. But you know that every man's strength is also his weakness. You need Jim's strong will and independence. You'd try to accommodate and please the whole world, if you could. Jim knows that, and he knows you wouldn't last very long if he didn't try to protect you from yourself.

Accept, Accept, Accept 53

"On the other hand, this same iron will could become the major cause of tension in your marriage. You must accept it in Jim. If you try to change him, you will only drive him away. He will become that much more stubborn and that much more independent."

So when I was single I accepted my loneliness before I could enjoy my freedom. In marriage I accepted my husband's weaknesses before I appreciated his strengths. As a mother I quickly realized that I had new areas of life to accept. Now I had to accept something far harder: myself. It was easier to accept others' mistakes than my own, to accept others' weaknesses, rather than mine. How could I accept the on-going reality of how far short I fell of the fictional mother image I had erected? I saw this ideal mother-figure exemplified by the beautiful television commercials showing the gentle mother joyously changing diapers and enjoying every moment of it.

I had dreamed of holding my baby for the first time. I could hardly wait to feel him suckle at my breast. But I had not counted on the feelings of rage and frustration and inadequacy that welled up within me when Jason wanted to nurse every hour on the hour. I never expected the oppressive burden of hearing him fuss and fuss, with no escape from his cries. Jason acted like a perfectly normal baby; I was a normal mother. But those facts didn't eliminate the feelings of inadequacy and guilt.

At times like this, Jim really helped. "Accept yourself, Sheila. [Had he been talking to mom, too?] You are not perfect. You're human. You will not always be the loving mother you should be. Sometimes you'll lose your patience and your temper. You may spank Jason, even though he doesn't deserve it. But that doesn't mean you're a failure as a mother.

"If you expect too much of yourself and aren't able to accept your shortcomings, then you do a great injustice to Jason. For when you don't forgive yourself and can't accept the fact that on occasion you're going to blow it, then you become depressed at your moments of weakness. A depressed mother is not a happy mother; a happy mother is all a baby needs."

You don't accomplish that easily. I wanted to be a perfect daughter, wife, and mother, but faced the impossible task of accepting my errors, blunders, and shortcomings. I made a commitment: I determined that for Jason's sake as well as my own, I would quit moping about and focusing on my mistakes. I took Jim's advice and accepted myself.

Accept Your Situation

My mother learned the principle of acceptance in the classroom before she was able to teach it. As a young girl she dreamed of becoming a concert organist. She spent every free hour away from the farm chores dashing off to the local church and practicing on the organ. She carefully saved her money for the day when she could leave home and study organ at college.

Everything was going as planned, until the war broke out. Her oldest brother was sent to fight in the Pacific. Her second-oldest brother went to Europe.

Accept, Accept, Accept

That left mom, who was next in line, to help with the remaining five children. It meant the postponement of her dreams of college and a career as an organist.

As she drove the tractor up and down the long, endless rows of hay, grandpa rode on the wagon behind her, tossing the bales into place. As he did, the hay dust clung to her hot, sticky skin, moist from the warm, humid air. Day after day, row upon row, she had to accept the fact that she was there in the field, or in the kitchen, or changing her baby brother's and baby sister's diapers, instead of pursuing her dream.

But if she had not accepted this unwanted change of plans, she would have been off at college that day when a young minister named Robert Schuller came to visit. He spotted mom immediately, and his practical mind quickly calculated that a pretty young organist would make the perfect minister's wife. After one date, he knew that she was the girl for him. Mother needed lots more convincing. After all, she didn't know what to think of this fiery young man who spun dreams of a church that sounded as though it belonged in another country.

Eventually dad's persistence paid off, and mom agreed to be his wife. But dad's offer was a package deal. Along with dad (who is a handful by himself), came the role of mother, wife, and first lady of his church.

With each of these roles came many lessons in the art of accept-ability. Her first lesson started when she and dad returned from their honeymoon to a parsonage miles from her home. Since her only experience away from home was the security of a college dorm, she took a frightening step.

The big city was a far cry from the bustling farmhouse, tucked safely away in the tiny village of Newkirk, Iowa. Suddenly she faced a lonely house in the middle of a teeming Chicago suburb.

Accept Others

As she had learned to accept her new home she had to accept the fact that her handsome husband minister was just as much a sinner as a saint. Her prince, she quickly discovered was just like other men, subject to imperfections and occasional insensitiveness.

Dad's humanity surfaced shortly after the newlyweds moved into their parsonage. Mom had carefully arranged the furniture the way she liked it and was sitting back, admiring it, when dad came home. My creative and opinionated father declared, "That looks all wrong, Arvella!" He proceeded to put things the way he thought they should be.

Well! This was not the way mom thought a husband should behave. According to her upbringing, home was the wife's domain. Why, husbands weren't even supposed to be *interested* in the way a home was decorated, much less *doing* the decorating!

Her new husband's interest and involvement in issues such as style, decor, furniture arrangements, and so on, were threatening to mother. Oftentimes she experienced inner hurt at dad's intrusion into what she considered her territory. However, she adopted a principle of accepting and adapting to her difficulties.

Accept, Accept, Accept 57

In learning to accept dad's weakness, she was free to see his strengths. When she accepted his sensitivity to his surroundings, she could value his design contributions to their home and to the churches in which they worked.

Accept Yourself

Over and over again I've seen mom survive in difficult situations and confront challenges by following the principle of acceptance. But her biggest battle has been in the area of self-acceptance. It took her many years to realize she is the successful wife and mother. Even so I'm sure she still doesn't recognize just how valuable she is to us all.

It is difficult for her to feel that she, a girl straight from the farm, could be an asset to a man like dad. Because she never completed a college education, she considered herself lacking in social graces, as well as intellectual pursuits. For a period in her life she seriously doubted her adequacy as a partner for her dynamic husband. At one time she even feared she was a hindrance to his ministry.

Those of us who really know the facts are aware that none of dad's work would have been possible if it had not been for mom. Her belief and support of his dreams gave him the courage to come to California and start an innovative form of worship: the walk-in, drive-in church. It was mother who accompanied him at the organ, week after week, year after year, until his church became today's thriving, international ministry.

In spite of all this, for my mother, self-acceptance has come slowly. Isn't it interesting that in this one area that caused my mother such deep concern, she constantly encouraged and affirmed me and sought to help me avoid the trauma she faced?

Have you ever thought, as I have, *If only I could be rid of my weaknesses, then everything would be peaches and cream*? That's not true, of course. In fact God teaches us, "In your weakness I am made strong. . . ." God says, "Sheila, when you are weak, then you will depend on Me. Then you will know Me better; then you will be able to serve Me better. Through your weakness, I can show you My tremendous love."

My mother taught me the importance of this beautiful paradox: Freedom comes from both relinquishment and dependence. In all areas of life, when we release our hold on people and things, even on tasks to be performed, we and they are set free. They can become the people of their own choosing. We can fulfill our responsibilities, while trusting in the sovereignty of our Heavenly Father.

Mother and I experience more and more of this on an on-going basis in our relationship with each other.

Part II

Between Mother and Daughter—Friendship

5

When a Mother Is a Friend

Out of the clear blue, my sixteen-year-old sister, Carol, complained, "I can't talk to mom! Whenever I try to share with her about a boy whom I like, she constantly harps on about him. Every time I leave the house she wants to know if *he's* going to be there. She wants to know if *he's* going to hold my hand or if *he's* going to drive me home. She drives me crazy!" Her eyes flashed angrily as she stomped off to her room, slamming the door behind her.

Had it been possible to follow Carol and observe her unaware, one probably would have witnessed an oft-repeated scene: Carol, flopped onto her bed, phone in hand, telling her best friend, Debbie, all about her latest crush.

Why is Carol able to share with Debbie, when she can't with our mother? It bothered me until I remembered how I acted when I was her age.

My friend, Peggy, and I—much like Carol and her friend, Debbie—used to spend hours in our rooms, talking about this guy or that one and how dreamy he was. These crushes, as well as other hopes and dreams and shared confidences, made our friendship special.

Would I have shared those same thoughts and feelings with my mother? No way! Not then! But things changed. That's because mom and I changed. And today we share openly, not just as mother and daughter, but as friends!

Moving Toward Friendship

How did this friendship of ours happen? How did I get from Carol's point to where I am today? What encouraged me to start opening up to mother, enabling the growth of an intimate and fulfilling friendship?

There was no overnight transformation. Our positive relationship developed over years. I believe every mother and daughter can experience a similar friendship, if mothers foresee and avoid the natural pitfalls that disrupt the relationship.

One pitfall is teenage withdrawal. The following chapter deals with this in more detail. But the way in which the mother handles her daughter's verbal and emotional silences will affect their future relationship. Consequently these silences must be handled carefully and sensitively.

When the mother clearly understands the mother-daughter relationship and the changes that will take place within it as the daughter grows and matures, she may easily avoid the pitfalls. Mothers of teenagers must recognize that the relationship they experience today will not always be this way. The wise mother anticipates the changes, the secure mother welcomes them, and the courageous mother guides as sensitively as she can the timing and manner in which the changes occur.

When a Mother Is a Friend

Birth begins the relationship as the mother simply transforms her ideas, teachings, and disciplines to her dependent, helpless, and ignorant infant. As the daughter begins to exert her first signs of independence their relationship increases in complexity. The baby exhibits her first signs of individualism within a few years as she grows into a young girl and eventually into a woman. During the process, the daughter extends her awareness of her own identity and needs, and she learns to meet those needs herself. This growth process varies from mother to mother and daughter to daughter. The degrees of freedom and discipline, as the daughter matures, differ greatly from family to family. But no matter how and when the shift occurs, the time comes when the mother and daughter are on the same level. The mother eventually chooses to no longer exert discipline over her daughter. If the maturation process progresses in the proper way at the right time, the mother and the daughter come to a point where they can relate to each other woman to woman, as friends.

The timing is crucial. I believe mothers make a big mistake when they give daughters the freedom to govern their own lives too early, before they have the wisdom and expertise to do so. Obviously the mother's ability to discern when to give her daughter freedom is a sensitive issue that each mother must settle within herself. But most high-school girls are not mature enough to live without parental boundaries such as curfews, which movies they can see, which parties they can attend. Mothers who think they are being buddies to daughters by allowing them to grow up in their own way or whenever they want to are actually playing with fire. The results are disastrous: First, the mother exposes her daughter to the risk of making an irreparable mistake that may cause her undue misery; second, chances are that the final relationship between the mother and daughter will never reach the full potential it could have had if the mother had acted more courageously in her role as disciplinarian.

It takes courage to say *no!* Afraid they won't be liked by their children, parents have been known to retreat from their disciplinary responsibilities, hoping to gain love. This results not in the love and admiration they desire, but in a lack of respect and much needed guidance.

The popular actress Dyan Cannon recently shared her ideas on the subject of mother-daughter relationships. She is the mother of a fifteen-year-old daughter. Both Dyan and her daughter, Jennifer, describe her as a *strict* mother. Jennifer frequently complains that "all the other kids get to do it."

Dyan's reply impressed me: "That's the way it is. Those are the rules. And this is tough. But if you're a loving person—and I am—and if you care about being loved—and I do—and if you love your daughter very much—and I do—when it comes to being a parent you have to risk them not liking you. They're not going to for a while, because you're the heavy. You're the one who stops them from staying out until 2:00 A.M. when everybody else can. But I'm telling you, it earns their respect and ultimately their friendship."

Wow! There's a lot of wisdom in that lady! Dyan is in tune with her role as mother. She knows that *for now* she must not give her daughter too much freedom too fast, lest she jeopardize Jennifer's future and their ultimate friendship. But Dyan feels the freedom to play the heavy because she knows that she won't have to all her life. Her relationship with Jennifer will change, and in just a few years she'll be able to shed her role as authoritarian.

Mothers can learn a lesson from Dyan. Teenage girls don't need another buddy or pal; they need a mother! When I was in high school, the term I would have used to describe my mother was just that: *mother,* not *friend.* I loved her, but I wouldn't have confided in her as I did in my girl friends. But I always respected her, even though there were times I resented all the rules.

Surrogate Mothers

It was during this time that I developed a friendship with Shirley Hinke. Shirley was an older woman who opened her home to teenagers. It was common, on weekends, to find as many as forty high-school students swarming throughout her house. At first I went to Shirley because of all the other kids who were there. But before long, the attraction extended to Shirley herself. She was a very loving, caring woman, and I found I could talk to her about anything and get excellent advice. I could tell her about my innermost feelings and even about my crushes.

Well, it wasn't long before I began to notice that my

friendship with Shirley was having repercussions at home. When I'd ask if I could go to Shirley's, mom would say, "Again?"

She was hurt. I had apparently chosen to love another woman, instead of her. But unless I had homework or some other pressing commitment, mother just sighed and said, "Okay. Go if you want to."

Although neither of us was aware of it at the time, and as threatening as it was to mother, the friendship with Shirley later proved to be a very important stepping-stone in the development of our mother-daughter friendship. Through Shirley I learned to share myself openly with a more mature woman, without fear of disciplinary repercussions. Her friendship brought positive wisdom to my life, without intimidation. For the first time in my life, I enjoyed a special woman-to-woman friendship.

My feelings toward mother changed very little when I was in high school, but when I suddenly found myself three thousand miles away from home, a freshman in college, our relationship changed drastically. For the first time in my life I was totally on my own. I answered only to me. Because I was no longer under my mother's authority, I began to relate to her woman-to-woman as I had to Shirley.

The friendship with Shirley Hinke proved invaluable. Later, when I worked as a counselor in the church's youth center, I found myself once more in relationships similar to the one I shared with Shirley: that of an older woman to a teenage girl. This time, however, at twenty-three years old, I was the older woman! My work showed me that this phenomenon of older friends or "surrogate mothers" is a common one among high-school girls. These relationships are always beneficial to the mother-daughter relationship, if the surrogate mother can provide a positive influence. The wise mother will not discourage the relationship, but will welcome it, even though there may be painful and threatening moments.

Surrogate mothers are most helpful during the teenage years, when the daughter feels an especially strong pull toward independence. Since the mother needs to retain her role as disciplinarian, the surrogate mother provides wisdom and a sample of real, mature friendship. Because the relationship with the surrogate is not related to parental discipline, the daughter feels free to confide her normal yet guilt-producing emotions to an adult. When the surrogate responds to these shared confidences with "That's normal; you're okay," the girl feels relief. In her newfound maturity she establishes a pattern on which to base a similar intimate friendship with her mother.

The Freedom of Friendship

Today mother and I share a deep, intimate friendship. Yet we do not limit our friendships to each other. Both of us have many other friends, and each relationship is as different as the personalities concerned.

The freedom to give ourselves to each other and to our friends results from our sense of personal self-acceptance. Security is essential in promoting healthy friendships between mothers and daughters. The lack of it not only drives a mother to a premature relinquishment of her responsibilities as her daughter's disciplinarian; it can also cause a mother to hold her child back in the process of maturation. Some mothers try to keep their daughters as little girls all their lives. Perhaps they fear that if they let them go, their girls will pass them by. Mothers can become jealous of their daughters, and jealousy is a natural by-product of insecurity.

True friends do not allow jealousy to destroy their relationship. A healthy spirit of competition may exist, but the green-eyed monster cannot come between friends, for it is more akin to hate than to love.

I recently met a woman who had grown up in an atmosphere of parental jealousy. Partly because this woman had a long history of mental illness, I was curious about her relationship with her mother. Although I discovered that her mother could not be blamed for all her problems, she must deal with one real problem in her relationship with her mother.

This middle-aged daughter remains a little girl, emotionally. Throughout her life, her mother, jealous of her pretty little girl, followed her with her authoritarian demands. The daughter never married, never held down a job, and today she lives with her mother. The result of the mother's selfishness was an emotionally crippled child. These women barely tolerate each other.

This case is extreme, but it shows that the roles between mothers and daughters must change, or bitterness, rebellion, and even hatred will result. However,

When a Mother Is a Friend

care must be taken that the change occurs only when the mother knows the daughter can accept the responsibilities and results that accompany her freedom.

Hope for the Future

If attaining a friendship with your mother or daughter sounds just short of impossible, remember this; when I ask the majority of my friends to describe their mothers in one word, the choice is almost unanimous: *friend!* Eventually most mothers and daughters reach the point in their lives when they are able to overcome past hurts, fears, and frustrations and are able to say, "She is my friend." This is God's plan for mothers and daughters. We need meaningful friendships as women.

So if you're a mother with a teenage daughter who gives no indication of affection toward you, don't dismay. Your relationship will bloom in time. And if you're a teenage girl who thinks your mother is the strictest ever, be glad she cares enough about you to be involved. The day will come when you will have the freedom you long for, though I hope it will not descend upon you before you are ready to handle its responsibilities.

No matter what your relationship seems like today, it is not the same as it was yesterday, nor will it be the same tomorrow. Give your friendship room to grow. Allow your mother or your daughter space for changes. Relish *all* your friendships.

For when we each, mothers and daughters, grow as individuals, we will be able to bring more and more to our friendship. Through my friendship with my husband, my sisters, my colleagues, as well as others, I contribute richly to the friendship I enjoy with my mother.

In the final analysis, no one brings anything to a friendship—*no one is able to be a friend—until she first makes friends with herself.* Self-friendship is the key to a vital relationship with anyone. God made it very clear when He told us, "Love your neighbor as yourself." He understood our need for self-love and self-affirmation as a prerequisite for all other loves. For only when you love yourself can you give yourself in love to others.

Where does one find this self-love? How does one discover the freedom to be a truly loving and caring friend? Shirley Hinke and my mother have found the secret. They are caring and loving women because they are first and foremost friends with Jesus. Through His love for them and for everyone they meet, they find the freedom and the fulfillment and the intimate love they share with me and many others.

6

Silence—Is It Always Golden?

"Silent. . . ."
"Withdrawn. . . ."
"In a shell. . . ."

When a mother uses these words to describe her teenage daughter, is there any hope at all for the friendship? Yes. Hope exists even for the mother and daughter who have a communication gap the size of the Grand Canyon.

Any mother handling the common problem of teenage withdrawal into silence faces a formidable task. The mother's ability to handle her daughter's silent phase can be pivotal to their future relationship. Depending on how well the mother understands and relates to the problem, she turns the relationship into a positive or negative vein.

Are there guidelines to help mothers through this time? Yes. Several mothers who handled it successfully, as well as those who admitted to making huge mistakes, offered the following suggestions:

1. *Do not try to* scare *your daughter into talking to you.* By that I mean don't push her or try to pry,

by means of fright, into the part of her world she shuts off from you.

2. *Do not* dare *your daughter to talk to you.* This point goes hand in hand with the first. Threats will achieve nothing in breaking through communication barriers.

3. *Do not* tear *yourself away from the problem* by running away from it, ignoring it, or by hoping it will go away by itself.

Rather: *Be* aware *of your daughter's feelings.* Look at her body language. Listen carefully to all the things she doesn't say, and you will be surprised at what you hear. *Be aware, but also,* share *your daughter's silences.*

What do I mean by *sharing*? I mean experience the silences with her. Don't let her go through them alone, but don't force yourself upon her. Be there, be aware, so when she feels ready, she will be able to share—this time, with you.

We can best learn about sharing by watching toddlers at play. Actually, their "play" resembles nothing more than a vigorous game of tug-of-war. As soon as one toddler sees the other toddler's toy, he thinks he *has* to have it. But mother can join in and help the children learn to share their toys. She says, "Johnny, you play with the truck, while Susie plays with the doll. After ten minutes are up, we'll switch toys." So the children take turns and learn early lessons in the art of sharing. As they do, a spirit of peace and harmony begins to spread through the room.

Silence—Is It Always Golden?

Sharing means "the ability to give and take." It means taking turns. In a child's terms, it is playing together peacefully.

It's the same in mother-daughter relationships. This particular sharing can be a real problem during the teenage years, when it seems as if the mother continually gives and the daughter always takes. How does a mother communicate and share with someone who doesn't want to give in return? How do you become friends with someone who won't share her life with you? How do you share with someone who won't even play the game, who locks herself in her room and totally shuts herself off in her private world of silence?

First, stop fighting it, and realize that you alone do not face this issue. Your problem is a common one. Teens typically withdraw from their families. If the mother learns not to overreact to her situation and not to be hurt by her daughter's silence, then the silent time benefits both.

Attempts to break through the daughter's communication barriers by force or manipulative methods lead to destruction. They only strengthen the barrier and weaken the relationship. Instead the mother should be aware of her daughter's need for silence as well as her need for mom to be there when she decides to reach out.

Realize that your daughter talks to you through her silence. Even though she may withdraw into a cocoon, woven with her bedroom, her radio, her friends, she is still crying out to you. Through the very act of withdrawal she probably says, "I am a person of my own now. I need to be respected for who I am: an individual. My feelings may not be mature, but nevertheless they are feelings, and as such they deserve to be treated with respect and tenderness." What then can a mother do? Just sit by and ignore the situation? No, but whatever you do, don't pry.

Trying to crack through the cocoon by negative methods, such as fright or threats, has an adverse affect. The parent who pushes his or her way into the teen's silence will only add brick and mortar to the walls between them.

I saw this very thing happen to many girls at the youth center. While working there, parent after parent came to me with the same complaint, "Make my kid talk to me!"

I never understood what made these parents think anybody could *make* their kids talk to them. How on earth could a stranger like me make a teen talk to her parents when she didn't want to? After all, any girl would be horribly embarrassed just to be in a counselor's office, not to mention that she'd be downright angry at the person who tried to drag her innermost thoughts out of her.

Beware of Daring

I'll never forget the father and mother who brought Rebecca to see me. This shy, sullen girl sat with her hands clasped nervously, her eyes riveted to the floor. Her parents, on the other hand, were angry. Their frustration reached the point of fury. The father got right to the point, "She won't talk to us."

Silence—Is It Always Golden?

"What do you mean, she won't talk to you? Doesn't she say *anything*?"

"No! Not a thing!"

Rebecca made no attempt to challenge her father's claim. He continued, "We told her that if she didn't start talking to us, we would take her to see a psychiatrist."

"I'm not a psychiatrist," I replied. "I'm only a youth counselor."

"Yeah, but you understand young people, don't you?"

"I do try to see life through their eyes, yes. Tell me, what prompted you to make such a threat to Rebecca?"

"Last night was the last straw. She's been saying less and less lately, but last night I'd had it. She sat there at the dinner table all night like a bump on a log. She wouldn't talk to us, so I said, 'Rebecca, how're you doing?' No response. Then I said, 'Rebecca, how's the food? Need any salt?' *Nothing!* Not even a shake of the head! Finally, I said, 'You're going to talk to me, or you're going to go to your room without anything else to eat!' You know what she did? Without so much as a word, she went to her room and stayed there all night!"

Rebecca's parents were angry victims of frustration. I understood their reactions when they resorted to threats and dares to try to make her open up, but they only made Rebecca retreat deeper into her shell. By the time they brought her to me, she was a very troubled girl who needed more help than I could give her.

Those first meetings with girls always seemed awkward. I usually felt nervous as I waited to meet a girl for the first time. I'd wonder: *What's she like? What does she need? Will I be able to help her?*

These first sessions never became easy; usually the girl didn't want to be there or felt embarrassed that she had to go to a counselor for help. The pathway to open sharing with these girls was a rocky one, to say the least. One day I happened upon a device that worked wonders.

My office, which doubled as the lounge for the youth workers in the evening, had a small coffee table in one corner. The leaders who had met there the night before had brought in a jigsaw puzzle to work while they took their breaks, between meetings.

It just so happened that I sat down at this coffee table with a girl I was meeting for the first time. As I asked my new acquaintance some routine questions, I noticed her fingers began to play with one of the puzzle pieces. Her eyes never met mine. Instead she busily searched for the home of her piece.

I took up her clue and began to work the puzzle with her. As we worked, I continued to ask her questions. I was amazed at the ease with which she answered me and the depth that our conversation reached. Never before had I experienced such a successful session.

The puzzle was the key. It gave the girl an excuse to avoid looking me in the eyes. Since eyes can tell more than we want them to, they can hinder the communication-barrier breakthrough. I decided the

Silence—Is It Always Golden?

puzzle would stay. I determined that as my girls put the pieces of the puzzle in place, I would try to help them with the puzzle of their lives.

Relationships and communication between mothers and daughters can often be a frustrating puzzle. My mother and I have experienced this feeling. Yet when one learns the basic principle of sharing the silences, doors of communication spring open.

One very important lesson we learn from the jigsaw puzzle is that, like the puzzle of the silences, you cannot force the pieces together, nor can you force the silence to go away. When two pieces do not fit, you can push all you want to, but they will not interlock. You will not make any progress in solving your puzzle by sheer force. The same is true in the mother-daughter relationship. You cannot force the sharing, the communicating, the giving and taking. You cannot pry into someone else's privacy.

You can guide each piece, each person, gently closer and closer, until you just snap into place. When the pieces are right, the time is right, the words are right, and the people are ready, then the pieces fit, and the intimate sharing takes place.

But do not expect it to happen overnight. Intimate friendship with a silent, withdrawn teenager takes years of gently being available.

Beware of Tearing

Mothers who lose patience with their daughters' silence and tear themselves away from the problem, by retreating into busy schedules, by ignoring it, or by just hoping that it will eventually go away by itself, suffer the same consequences as those who try to scare or dare their daughters into talking to them. The mother's unwillingness to deal with the daughter's withdrawal only makes the gap wider. Her retreat appears to the daughter as indifference, and the daughter thinks her mother's interests and schedules are far more important than she is. Certainly no daughter shares with someone who appears not to care.

The other day, I discussed these thoughts with a friend of mine, Ruthe Messenger. She interrupted me, saying, "Sheila, let me tell you how I handled my children's silent times." Whenever one of her two children had been too quiet, Ruthe would sit on that child's bed and occupy herself with a quiet pastime. She would ask, "You don't mind if I just sit here for a while, do you?" They usually mumbled, "No." As they continued to study, read, or listen to their records Ruthe just sat there silently, occupying herself. Often hours would go by without anyone saying a word. Sometimes Ruthe's time was just a time of silence shared between a mother and child. On other occasions, her son or daughter would turn to her and say, "Mom, things aren't going too well...." So they would begin to share.

Patience and gentleness are two very important qualities that promote the solution to communication puzzles between mothers and teenage daughters. How many of us are willing to just sit for hours, maybe even years, waiting to give our daughters the opportunity to share, willing to give them the time they need

Silence—Is It Always Golden?

until they feel ready to talk?

This kind of reaction takes a tremendous amount of love and care, especially in a day when mothers are busy and have a good deal of pressure on them. A child may easily feel in second place. Who wants to share her inner feelings with someone if she doesn't really know those feelings will be treated with care?

The results of a mother's not being available when the daughter *is* ready to share can be disastrous. As with the puzzle, merely looking at the problem never solves it. In solving the puzzle, you have to pick up the pieces. To break the silence, you have to make yourself available to your daughter. If you turn your back on her now, you may never experience this intimate friendship.

Be Aware and Share the Silences

Like most teenagers, I went through silent times. Although I could talk to mother about some of my problems, I buried the real hurts inside myself because they hurt too much to discuss.

At six feet tall in my stocking feet, I felt very awkward. I acquired six inches of growth in less than two years' time. Although I had been on eye level with all my friends when summer vacation started, in the fall I returned to school to tower over everyone—even the boys! When I looked in the classroom windows, I saw a group of high-school girls mirrored there. But one stood out like a giant: me!

I felt like a freak.

To compensate for my height, I began to stand with

all my weight on one hip, with my other leg stretched out. I looked about an eighth of an inch shorter, had a twisted profile, and a foot that got in everybody's way.

I use to spend hours wondering how I could make myself shorter. In teen magazines I read about girls who had sections of their legs removed to make them shorter. If it hadn't sounded so painful, I probably would have considered it. Instead I took to a less painful method: slouching. I rounded my shoulders as much as I could, pulled my stomach in, and tried to shrink my body by the way I stood.

Of course it really didn't do any good: The result was just a six-foot slouch! Comments from strangers didn't help at all. Frequent remarks like, "Man, you're tall," made me feel like a carnival sideshow. The stares people gave me when I first got up, up, up from my chair, made me want to sit down and never get up again.

Although I never discussed my problem with my mother, she was aware of it. During shopping trips, she saw my dismay at the lack of selection of shoes without three-inch heels or at pants that came to mid-calf. She noticed the glum look of depression that hung around me suddenly and the rounded, insecure shoulders of a teenager who felt too tall to be wanted. But I did not verbally share my feelings with her, for it hurt too much to put into words. Besides, I assumed I was a disappointment, not only to my friends, but also to my mother.

But mom listened to my cries through my silence, through my slouched shoulders, through the body language that just reeked with insecurity. Rather than

Silence—Is It Always Golden?

trying to pry the feelings out of me, one night, just out of the blue, she said, "Sheila, you're a beautiful girl, you know." I burst into a torrent of tears. "I am not! I'm tall and ugly, and no one wants to be my friend because I'm so tall. I'm nothing but a freak!"

She just continued as calmly and gently as she could, "Models are tall." But I replied, "Yeah, yeah! I know all about that. But models are skinny, too, and I'm definitely not skinny! I'm just *big!*"

Although it seemed mom had failed to help me, her words made an impact. She didn't stop, but continued to tell me that I wasn't a freak, that I wasn't abnormal, and that I could be beautiful.

Mother affirmed and challenged me. She told me to stand up straight! She made me put down that candy bar. She encouraged me to hold my head up high and reminded me that true beauty dwells within. Finally she convinced me I wasn't a freak, when she said, "Sheila, you are unique. There's only one Sheila, and I think she's pretty special."

Nothing my mother could do would make me shorter, but mom shared my feelings of insecurity and helped me see beyond them. She did not try to force her way into my life through fright or threats, but I opened up to her positive words of love.

She stayed there during the silence; she tuned into it and listened to what I was saying through my body language. In this way, she heard what I was feeling, when I couldn't express it verbally.

Bear in mind that my mother did not meet with success at the beginning. Many times her words fell on deaf ears. Many times I stormed away from her, shut myself off in my room, threw myself across the bed, and cried for hours. But eventually her love and patience got through. Eventually I saw the beauty God created in me.

The silence in my life, as in many other teens' lives, was a symptom of the hurt I experienced. For other daughters, the withdrawal indicates the process of establishing independence and personal identity. Whatever the causes, this silence causes pain in the heart of a caring mother. But if she is wise, she will remember that she only needs to be there, be aware, and finally, to share not only her daughter's words, but also the silences.

7

Dream a Little Dream With Me

What makes up the special relationship between friends? Carol and Debbie, Peggy and I, and mom and I have all experienced the elements of friendship. But what *are* friends? Two persons who share: words and silences, hopes and fears, successes and failures, dreams and discouragements.

For the patient mother the time will come when her daughter has grown through the silent phase, and from behind the closed door has emerged a woman ready to share her dreams. Then friendship blooms, extending both ways. Soon both mother and daughter are sharing with each other hopes, fears, and dreams.

My family regards dreams as precious commodities to be treasured, nurtured, and highly valued. We handle every dream with utmost care because its death would be a tragedy. Discouragement kills dreams, but a word of encouragement can help them come true. Here is my firsthand experience.

When I was twenty-five I dreamed of being married. It's not easy to admit that marriage is a dream when you are single, with no positive dating prospects. As years went by I became so discouraged that I finally approached mother with my hurt.

"What's wrong with me? How come I can't find a man who loves me the same way dad loves you?"

"You will, Sheila," she said, trying to encourage me. "You will."

"Aw, come on. What makes you say that? I mean, I'm already twenty-seven years old."

"I just believe you will get married someday. I don't really know why I believe that, but I do. You're a special young woman, and you deserve a special young man. God will bring him into your life when the time is right and when both of you are right."

Until my mother said, "... when the time is right and when both of you are right," I felt discouraged and was quickly becoming a negative, bitter person. Suddenly I began to see the light. My dream for marriage and a happy family hadn't died; it just wasn't time for it to come true yet. For a reason that only God knew, my dream had to wait a while. I took heart and began to believe again.

My biggest problem, as Grandma Schuller put it, was that I was so picky. She said to me one day, in her usual blunt manner, "Sheila, how do you expect to find a mate if you won't accept a date?"

A mate? My mind screamed in horror. *I don't want a mate! I want a man who will love me the way my father loves my mother.*

The crux of my problem was that my father is the kind of man every woman dreams of: exciting, handsome, one who treats my mother regally. It seemed impossible that I could find such a man.

But I refused to settle for anything less. As my

mother said, "There's a man who's perfect for you, Sheila. I just know it. When the time is right, God will bring the two of you together."

He did it in a way that surprised me. I met Jim at age twenty-four. He came to the church to work as the head of the art department. He brought along his brushes and art boards, a long ponytail, and a bright red Porsche. The church couldn't help but notice him! Yet in his own, mysterious way, he kept to himself most of the time. When I finally got up the courage to talk to him, I discovered a really nice guy.

I grew to love Jim as a friend. Our totally different natures made romance look impossible. It never entered our minds. For four years our friendship grew, and we grew.

Jim's daily exposure to positive Christian faith changed his views on life. Pretty soon the ponytail was gone and the mustache shaved off. Jim smiled more frequently and readily. In our sharing I could see he had greatly changed from the man I met four years earlier. He now loved Jesus Christ.

One day, after meeting with him over a brochure that he was designing for me, I found myself thinking about him. As I recalled the things he said and the change in his life-style, he casually strolled by my desk. When he did, I suddenly saw him through different eyes. I saw him for the first time as a handsome man. To my utter surprise my heart went reeling and falling—head over heels in love.

The new feelings were exhilarating, but terrifying. I went to my mother, now as a friend, to share my feelings. I knew my mother would treat my dream carefully and that I could count on getting the encouragement I needed. I feared the pain that could result from my allowing myself to continue to hope there could ever be anything between Jim and me. I needed to have the courage to believe and to hang in there, rather than running away from a beautiful dream.

When I shared my feelings with my mother, she was delighted. "I like Jim!"

"But I'm so scared. We've been friends for four years, and he's never asked me out before. Why should he now?"

"Maybe the time wasn't right. Maybe both of you weren't right. Perhaps now everything is right!"

Mother knew best. Apparently the time *was* right, for Jim soon asked me to go out for coffee with him. After only a few dates I knew Jim was everything a woman could want; so when he asked me to be his wife, I joyfully accepted.

I do not doubt that the story would have had a less-than-happy ending if I had not managed to be victorious over my moments of despair and discouragement. I derived the strength I needed, during those difficult times, from friends like my mother, but mostly from Psalms 37:4: "Commit your way to the Lord . . . and he will give you your heart's desires."

God encouraged me through those verses. When you are in tune with Him and His desires for your life, then *His* desires become *your* desires and vice versa. If you let God guide you in all matters, then you can be assured that no matter how impossible it may seem,

Dream a Little Dream With Me

God will grant you your desires in His time, or else He will change your feelings and lead you to the point where you no longer have the desire.

Dreaming God's Dreams

God is a loving God. He never teases. He will not plant a desire within you only to frustrate and hurt you. If you follow God and have committed your way to Him, then you must believe that your dream is from Him and that He will use it to bring you closer to His beautiful plan for you.

For these reasons the verses from Psalms gave me the courage to believe in my dreams and to encourage others to believe in theirs. It's not easy for mothers to encourage daughters. They fear that the higher they build up their hopes, the harder they can fall.

That concern is legitimate, although misplaced. Actually the mother overlooks a far more important matter: Is the daughter, as well as the mother, walking in God's way? Are both committed to His plan for their lives? Do they know God loves them and only wants what's best for them? He does. He also says: "I have a plan for you. It is a plan for good and not for evil, to give you a future with hope!"

When the mother and daughter believe that beautiful promise, then there is reason to hope, no matter how impossible the dream seems. When we walk close to God, hope can dwell in our hearts; for God always has a very specific purpose in giving us our dreams, though that purpose may not be made clear for a long time.

I learned to trust God's guidance in a roundabout way. From the time I was seven years old, it had been my dream to become a doctor. As soon as I was old enough, I began to take every class I could to help make my dream a reality. In high school, my science classes seemed simple enough, but college was another matter. I suddenly found myself nearly eaten alive by such monsters as physics, chemistry, and biology. Science suddenly ceased to be a fascinating view of life. Instead it was hard, torturous work!

Throughout the difficult years of studying, my parents continually encouraged me. They gave me the courage to keep on trying when I wanted to quit. Through their loving affirmation I risked failure and the accompanying disgrace. Through the experience, I realized the real meaning of the word *encourage*. In my book it means "to give courage through love. To reaffirm to the one who is disheartened, because you will love him no matter whether his dreams die or thrive."

I managed to keep going and keep studying the whole four years. My grade-point average was good enough to give me the hope of admittance to medical school, yet low enough to make my senior year a nervous one.

As I waited for the schools to reply to my applications, I realized that the moment of truth had arrived. Depending on the replies, my lifelong dream would be fulfilled or killed. In this frame of mind I watched my father on "Hour of Power," as I did every Sunday when I was away at school. On one particular Sunday,

Dream a Little Dream With Me

dad's words had a life-changing impact on my thinking.

He said, "Success is not fame or fortune or recognition. Rather, success is being the person God wants you to be. It is finding a hurt and healing it; it is helping people discover their own self-worth and showing them how they in turn can help others."

I realized that all those years, my dream of being a doctor had been tainted with desires for fame and recognition. Maybe I had been pursuing *my* dream for my life, not *God's*. Perhaps He had something else in mind.

As I became aware of the possibility that I had been pursuing the wrong dream, an interesting thing happened. My mother came to mind. Certainly she could not be considered a famous person. Why, only a handful of people know how faithfully she serves the church and how diligently she works night after night to help dad. Most of her behind-the-scenes work would not gain much recognition. But without it, the ministry would fold. Without mom, dad is nothing.

Mother's work is *vital*. She saves lives just as surely as does any emergency-room doctor. Through her contribution to the "Hour of Power," she has saved the emotional lives of millions of people.

I decided then and there that I wanted my life to count for God. I wanted to do anything that He wanted me to do. I prayed, "Lord Jesus, take my life. Use it. Help me be the woman You want me to be. Show me Your dream for my life."

When I finished my prayer, I felt at peace with myself and my God. I knew He was in control of my life, and I couldn't think of anyone who could take better care of me. I was prepared for any reply from the medical schools—even the rejections.

Indeed it was providential that I had that experience with God before they came, for come they did—one rejection after another. It hurt to hear, time after time, that I wasn't good enough, but I believed and trusted that my future was in God's hands. I knew I had done my best, and that was all that He asked of me.

When my last rejection arrived in the mail, I called my parents to tell them the news. Mother answered the phone. As she listened to me casually tell her I would not be continuing my medical studies, she began to cry softly. "Oh, Sheila, I'm so sorry. I know how much it meant to you."

"It's okay, mom. Really. I had a long talk with God about it, and I know that I am living in His will for my life. I truly believe He has something else in mind for me. And you know what? The funny thing is, I don't think I want to be a doctor anymore: It's an *awful lot of work!*"

My dream was transformed that day, when I no longer had the desire to pursue medicine. That's what God does when our lives are in His control, when we commit our dreams to Him. He helps us grow through our difficult times, as painlessly as possible. My desires became His desires. God did not desire me to be a physician.

Do I regret the years of hard work for nothing? No, because I don't believe that they were for nothing. I

Dream a Little Dream With Me

don't believe God wanted me *to be* a doctor, but I do believe that He wanted me to *pursue* medicine. Why? Because the act of pursuing that rigorous field of study gave me something nothing else would have: character.

My pursuit shaped my character during my teen years. When all my friends floundered, seeking their vocations, I knew where I wanted to go and what I wanted to do. That made my choices simple. I chose to stay home and study. I chose to stay out of trouble. By the time my dream changed, my character was established, and I had laid strong foundations that are mine forever.

My parents' words of encouragement were not in vain. They gave me the courage to try something I never would have attempted otherwise. If I had never pursued medicine, I would wonder all my life if I missed out on something I really wanted to do. Now I know: It's not for me.

Dare to Hope

When my mother encouraged me, she did not give me false hope. Even when I encountered difficult classes that all but overwhelmed me intellectually, my mother encouraged me. When she did, she was not leading me on. She merely wanted me to give until I didn't *want* to give anymore. When I finally failed to get into medical school, I successfully handled the rejections. I emerged from the whole experience a stronger and better woman.

Some mothers fear to encourage their daughters,

because they might give them false hope. By restraining their encouragement, they feel they do them a good deed, that they spare their daughters heartbreak. In actuality these mothers hurt their daughters. By discouraging our children from following their dreams, we only stifle their potential and stunt their emotional growth.

In my vocabulary, there is no such thing as *false hope*. That phrase must have been invented by a negative-thinking expert who never understood the meaning of faith. Some people have to have all the facts in front of them before they can "believe." This kind of person is incapable of believing; he limits himself to knowing.

If people needed to understand everything before they dared step out and try something new, no one would ever have discovered America; we'd still think the world was flat, and miles of the western world would be barren wasteland.

We need the same sort of courage in our personal relationships. Mothers need to believe in themselves and their daughters. We must encourage each other to dream dreams that have world-shaking potential. Until we do, we limit ourselves to mediocrity. Our lives remain average, and we develop less than our ultimate capabilities. Everyone can choose excellence. If we believe in ourselves and live our lives to the hilt, we know that there is no such thing as a hopeless situation; with God all things are possible.

If anyone had reason to lose hope, Toby and Barb Waldowski did. Recently late one night they called

Jim and me, requesting prayer. They'd just discovered that they might never be able to have children. Barb was scheduled for surgery in the morning, because she appeared to have cysts on both ovaries.

I could hear the tears in Barb's voice as she told us, and I knew how much having children meant to her. Jim and I prayed for her that night.

The next morning, when I went to the hospital, Toby told me Barb had not had ovarian cysts. The Fallopian tube openings were blocked, but the doctors had been able to do a relatively simple operation to correct her condition through surgery. They had told him she probably could get pregnant in about six months.

Toby and Barb jubilantly planned for and dreamed of the day when they would bring the baby home. But six months passed into a year. During that time, Barb thought several times that she was pregnant, but each time she went in for a pregnancy test, it came out negative. Her rising hopes crashed each time.

When I became pregnant with Jason, Barb generously shared my joy. As I carried and gave birth to him, she remained as excited as if she'd been my sister.

One day Barb called with even worse news: While the doctors had been testing Toby for infertility, they had discovered testicular cancer.

"Barb," I said. "You know it's possible that God has allowed you to remain infertile in order to discover this tumor early enough to save Toby's life."

"Yes, that's true," she replied. "Oh, Sheila! I don't

care if I have children. I just want my Toby!"

After much crying and praying we left it in the hands of One stronger than us.

The tumor was removed, and weeks of radiation followed. One day my phone rang. Barb excitedly told me that when she had gone for more infertility tests, the pregnancy test the doctor had routinely run was, surprisingly, positive. She was pregnant! I don't remember ever hearing such good news. All the words of encouragement I gave her through her trials had been well worth the effort. I had told her that God had planted the desire in her heart, and He would grant it when the time was right. And He did. Nine months later a beautiful healthy little Jesse Waldowski found his way into many hearts.

All things are possible with God! There is no such thing as false hope when you believe in an omnipotent God!

We mothers and daughters need to encourage and believe in each other. Some days mom needs to build me up, and other days it's the other way around. But we must never be afraid to say an encouraging word for fear that we will falsely lead someone on.

Undoubtedly this philosophy of hope requires faith in a loving God who can work miracles and turn seemingly impossible situations around and who can soften hard-as-stone hearts. My mother and I are free to encourage our friends because we share this faith. We not only believe in a powerful God who can do anything He feels is right, but we also believe in a caring God who guides us in all our decisions. My mother and

Dream a Little Dream With Me

I have committed our lives to God's care. We believe He will only allow those things in our lives that will ultimately be for our good. That doesn't mean He will necessarily spare us from hurt, for pain can help us to grow into the women He ultimately wants us to be.

Therefore when mom comes to me and shares a dream, I cannot say, "Hey! I don't think you should dream that dream. Why you might fail and get hurt if you do!"

What I can say is, "If this is what you think God wants you to do, I'm behind you all the way. Sure there's risk involved, but where isn't there? I believe in you! Try it! Go for it!"

Encourage each other. Share each other's dreams, hopes, fears, and frustrations. After all, what are friends for?

Part III

Between Mother and Daughter— Love

8

Love Expects and Accepts

Love is very patient and kind, never jealous or envious, never boastful or proud, never haughty or selfish or rude. Love does not demand its own way. It is not irritable or touchy. It does not hold grudges and will hardly even notice when others do it wrong . . . If you love someone you will be loyal to him [or her] no matter what the cost. You will always . . . expect the best of him [or her] and always stand your ground in defending him [or her].

1 Corinthians 13:4, 5, 7 TLB

Wow! If this is a true and accurate definition of love, then is motherly love possible? I mean, how many mothers can say they have never been irritable or touchy? Who can say that she has never lost patience with her children? I can't!

Why, just this morning I lashed out at Jason for spilling a whole box of bobby pins on the bathroom floor. Then he managed to get the box of Cheerios off the table and pour them over the bobby pins. By the time I found him, he had ground the Cheerios and the bobby pins into a crumbly pulp. I confess I became irritable and touchy. Yes, I noticed how naughty he had been. In fact my reaction to the sight was neither patient nor kind.

I know I'm not the only mother who experiences such unloving moments with her children. The other day I heard my neighbor being impatient when her toddler tried flushing his Tonka truck down the toilet.

Is there hope for mothers? What is the Bible saying to us about love? Many people cite these verses as their favorite—even mothers.

I, too, have always enjoyed this passage in 1 Corinthians. The thoughts are nice, and the words are pretty. I suppose that's why so many couples choose to have it read at their weddings. But for all the times I've read it or heard it recited, it never had the impact on me that it had today.

I suppose my state of mind this morning was still being affected by the Cheerios–bobby-pin scenario. For as I read the preceding verses, they suddenly didn't sound as nice and pretty as they had before. Instead, this thought jumped out at me: *If this definition of love is true and if you believe the Bible is true— which I do—then all mothers are doomed to a life of imperfect loving.*

Let me prove it to you. Take the following test, and answer the true-false questions *honestly*. (For those of you who are tempted to cheat, I have inserted extra checkpoints in parenthesis beside the "incorrect" answers.)

Love Expects and Accepts 101

	True		False
1. I have always been patient with my children.	☐	(How old is your baby?)	☐
2. I have never been envious of my brothers or sisters or friends.	☐	(Are you an only child?)	☐
3. I have never been boastful to an in-law.	☐	(Single?)	☐
4. I have never been selfish in the way I treated my husband.	☐	(Ditto.)	☐
5. I have never held a grudge.	☐	(Not even that time when you gave that extra-special gift to a friend who never thanked you?)	☐
6. I have never noticed when my husband made a mistake.	☐	(*Who* did *you* marry?)	☐

If you answered *False* to any or all of the above questions, then you'll have to agree—no one is able to love *perfectly!*

Did you ever think about that before? *No one*—not you, not your mother, absolutely no one—is capable of loving *perfectly, all the time.* We humans are imperfect as lovers, as well as in every other area of our lives.

I don't know about you, but I sure am relieved to know that I'm not the only one who isn't able to love perfectly all the time. I sure am glad to understand the fact that my imperfection in loving doesn't negate my love. Just because I get upset with Jason doesn't mean I don't love him; it just means I'm imperfect; I'm human!

It's a relief to realize that this biblical definition of love is a description of *perfect* love. God does not intend to frustrate us, for He knows we will fall short of the definition time and again. He wants us to have an ideal toward which we can grow. He wants to give us guidelines. He provides us with a tool with which to examine ourselves and see—not where we've failed, but where we can improve!

Upon examination of this love passage in 1 Corinthians, one concept stands our glaringly: "Love believes the best." Mothers could concentrate their attention here. This one facet of love is often overlooked: "Love believes the best."

This concept means a great deal to me because I was raised in a home where a great deal of emphasis was placed on possibility thinking and the power of positive expectations. My parents always expect us children to do and be our best.

Love Assumes the Best

Because of this emphasis in my upbringing, a recent article in *Parents'* magazine captured my attention: "Expectations—A Key to Development." The article shared the finding of two physicians from the University of Washington: "Infants whose mothers expected them to learn at a very early age developed more quickly than those of whom less was expected. Presumably, the mother who has higher expectations for her child tends to stimulate the child more, thus fostering development."

Simply stated, parental expectations can determine who and what children become. If mothers expect their daughters to become beautiful, successful, lov-

Love Expects and Accepts

ing, and caring women, then the chances are very high that they will become precisely that. Conversely if we assume they will be troublesome, insecure, and hardened, then they very likely will be like that.

To help mothers learn how to cultivate positive expectations for their daughters, I've divided "Love believes the best" into three distinct phases. They are:

1. Love assumes the best
2. Love approves the best
3. Love accepts the rest

Mothers must approve the best and accept the rest as well as assume the best. How does this work?

Love Approves the Best

Positive reinforcement goes hand in hand with a mother's postive expectations for her daughter. When a child accomplishes what the parent expected, that fact should be acknowledged. Child psychologists discovered that acknowledgment is a key to developing self-esteem. They now say you never can start too early. The parent who claps for her toddler who gets down from a chair by herself or drinks from a cup without drowning herself acknowledges and approves of the child's accomplishments.

The same psychologists carefully emphasize that parents should reinforce only good behavior and true accomplishments. Approval for its own sake does *not* promote healthy self-esteem. Empty praise accomplishes nothing. Yet it is a temptation to heap empty praises on delightful toddlers who so enthusiastically respond to approval.

Take Jason, for example. When I clap for my son, his face lights up with a brilliant smile. He starts clapping, too. His happiness shines out of his face. But toddlers grow up. Most children quickly become embarrassed by adulation and only reluctantly show pleasure that their accomplishments have been noticed, much less admired. The wise mother will not withhold praises when her daughter displays outward indifference to appreciation. Instead mom looks beyond the facade, to see the beaming child in her daughter.

According to the experts, a delicate balance must be struck in giving approval. For me the choice is clear. If I must err as a mother—which I will—let it be on the side of approval. I would rather have others accuse me of praising my children too much than too little.

Maternal approval is vital to the development of the daughter's healthy sense of self-esteem. The daughter who does not receive enough seeks it until she finds it. If approval is consistently out of reach, she will soon seek attention, instead. Approval, which results from positive actions, is the much healthier of the two. The results of the daughter's search for attention could hurt her.

Surprisingly, this need for approval never goes away. To some extent every maturing daughter continually seeks it. Although I am a mother myself, I feel the urge to share my latest accomplishments with mother.

I suspect that I am not alone, but am just one of many such grown approval seekers. I base these sus-

Love Expects and Accepts

picions on a remark made recently at a special embroidery class I was taking. After the teacher demonstrated a particularly dazzling new stitch, one middle-aged student said, "Wait until I show my mother!"

Whether the daughter unabashedly displays her need for approval or claims that it doesn't matter what her mother thinks of her, the truth is this: Deep down all daughters long for their mother's approval. So much so, in fact, that some daughters would rather ditch a dream than risk a scene. Some women will abandon a pursuit rather than meet with maternal disapproval.

Let me illustrate what I mean by sharing a seemingly insignificant experience that occurred over twenty-three years ago.

I was seven years old and furious! "Please, mom," I pleaded. *"Please* let me go to Sue's."

"No. It's almost supper time."

"Aw, mom. There's a whole hour left before dinner. *Please* can I go? Just for a little while?"

"Okay, go!" she declared harshly.

Her anger surprised me as much as the fact that she'd given me permission. For some strange reason, I suddenly lost the desire to go.

"Why are you just standing there, Sheila? I thought you were dying to go to Sue's."

"Yeah, well—I guess I changed my mind."

Mom shook her head, as much bewildered as I was by the whole scene.

I wasn't able to make any sense of it until just recently. What really happened was this: Mom had given me her permission, but not her blessing. Without her blessing, I did not feel free to pursue my goal, which was to go to Sue's.

The mother who seeks to develop her daughter's self-esteem and love between herself and her daughter will remember to *approve the best!*

Love Accepts the Rest

What is the "rest"? It is all those less-than-the-best things that can't be changed, including efforts that don't match up to our expectations, attempts that have failed, and physical attributes that are unattractive or at least less than desirable. God wants us to pursue love that can accept the unacceptable, love that accepts ugliness as well as beauty and failures as well as successes.

When a mother can see beyond her daughter's imperfect attributes and when the daughter can accept her mother's moments of failure, then they experience the blossoming of a rare love. This God-inspired love is the beautiful goal all mothers and daughters should strive for.

This love for others will not happen until the mother and daughter first learn to love themselves. They must assume the best about themselves, approve the best in themselves, and accept the rest of themselves.

The first two seem to be easier than the third, so it has been for me. My greatest difficulty has been accepting something I used to think was far from best: my height, all six feet of it.

Love Expects and Accepts

I cannot change my height. I can slump to one hip when I stand, or I can sit in a chair all evening, but the fact remains: When I stand, I am six feet tall. Today I have learned that I can fight it or "kite" it. I like the idea of kiting, being carried above the negatives, where you can clearly see the positives. When I kite my height, suddenly I am carried to new dimensions where I catch new sights of myself—inside and out.

At one time I did not rise above my unchangeable feature; it overcame me. To me feminine women were petite. Therefore I felt I had failed as a woman and a daughter; I feared that mom longed for a little, frills-and-lace daughter. When I looked in the mirror I feared that I was a deep disappointment to her.

Years later I shared my secret fear with my mother, only to find she had never felt that way. She accepted my height, but I had to deal with my attitude toward it. Through years of loving and patient acceptance from my mother, I began to see the beauty in my height. I changed my attitude.

The well-known "Serenity Prayer" helped me in my acceptance. You have heard it, I'm sure: "God grant us the serenity to accept the things we cannot change, the courage to change the things we can, and the wisdom to know the difference."

You or your loved ones may have traits you wish that you could change, but can't. Love accepts them and helps the ones we love to accept them. Love does not resent the ugly features or the unattractive characteristics or the apparent failures. Rather, it raises them to a higher dimension. Love sees life from God's perspective. When viewed from there, it is easier to accept the less-than-perfect that can be found anywhere in life. Even the dark aspects of life appear beautiful, when seen from God's view.

As one poet said:

> My life is like a weaving between my God
>   and me,
> I do not choose the colors, He worketh
>   steadily.
> Ofttimes He weaveth sorrow and I in foolish
>   pride,
> Forget He sees the upper, and I the
>   underside.

How important it is for us to image the rich tapestry God is making out of our lives.

Our lives, like tapestries, are woven with many different colored threads, including blues, reds, black, and gold. All together the colors make up one picture. Like any needlework viewed from the back, the picture is blurred by the knots. But when viewed from the right side, the picture comes clear. If you look carefully, you will see that the black threads are just as important as the gold ones. Without either, the picture would not be as beautiful.

So it is with love between mothers and daughters. Mothers can strive to assume the best, approve the best, and accept the rest, but none of us will always do it perfectly. Sometimes your love for each other will not shine very brilliantly. There may be days when the feeling of love does not exist at all between mother and

Love Expects and Accepts

daughter. On other days intimacy will draw the two of you together in a beautiful emotional experience.

If we look at our relationships, as well as ourselves, from the human point of view, they can look like a mess, like the back of a tapestry. But if we remember that the black days are as important as the gold ones and we ask God to grant us the grace to see ourselves from His point of view, we may be amazed at the beauty of the picture we are creating!

9

Love Respects

> Love is ... never jealous or envious, never boastful or proud, never haughty or selfish or rude. Love does not demand its own way....
> 1 Corinthians 13:4, 5 TLB

"Love is never.... Love does not...."

At first these verses appear to describe what love *isn't*. Yet if we examine them closely, we can also see what love *is*. One phrase capsulizes the love described in these verses: *Love is respect!*

Substitute *respect* for the word *love* in the above passage. It reads: "Respect is never jealous or envious, never boastful or proud, never haughty or selfish or rude. Respect does not demand its own way." The message rings out clear: Love respects!

Respect has become a much overlooked commodity these days. We all sense a definite trend toward selfishness in our society. We see this in self-help books and the advice of some psychologists. Both urge people to watch out for themselves, to assert their own ideas, and to pursue individuality. Everyone needs to pursue these goals to a certain degree, but they must be tempered with respect for others' needs, ideas, and personhood.

Love Respects

When the experts ignore these needs, many self-centered people emerge. Our society has lost its sense of balance and has swung so far toward individualism and me-ism that individuals have lost their sensitivity to others needs and feelings. The results are shown in rampant divorce rates and the dissolution of countless families.

Nobody wins when respect goes by the board. Selfishness leads to failure in relationships as well as in business. No woman succeeds at anything unless she learns genuine concern for others. If she wants to be a winner, she must heed this warning: *Assertiveness without respect does not equal success.*

These attitudes affect mother-daughter relationships. A deluge of recently published literature addresses this subject. Many authors urge daughters to be independent and assertive. Most neglect to balance their statements with a plea to daughters to retain respect for their mothers.

Where does one draw the line? Certainly daughters need to feel free to develop into mature women and to express their individuality. Yet they should not flippantly toss aside their mothers' ideals and teaching in the pursuit of independence.

You cannot disregard the values and concerns of others because they differ from yours. To completely ignore and rebel against the ideas of an older, more mature woman is not merely disrespectful; it can be disastrous. Every ideal deserves consideration, and every person is worthy of respect.

Every action does not deserve admiration: Some

mothers make moral decisions that degrade both mother and daughter. They blatantly disregard the principles of commitment and moral values. Mothers make genuine mistakes of all kinds. It is not necessary that daughters agree with *all* their mothers' decisions and actions. But when a mother is truly repentant, she should receive her daughter's love, forgiveness, and—yes—respect.

All mothers merit respect and admiration as persons. Most are entitled to respect and admiration as women who have a great deal of wisdom.

Daughters need to maintain respect for their mothers while pursuing the goal of independence. But this kind of esteem is not a one-way street; mothers do not have the market cornered. Daughters merit respect, too. Their ideas, hopes, and pursuits, no matter how foolish they seem, must be respected by their parents. Nothing kills a child's spirit faster than ridicule. Nothing thwarts a daughter's ability to respect herself and her dreams faster than lack of consideration from her parents.

Any dream deserves esteem. Any person who dares to dream should be treated with the highest admiration. The mother who laughs at her daughter's dreams or disregards her need for individualism pushes her ideas on her daughter; when she fails to let her child decide some things for herself, a woman destroys her daughter's spirit and extinguishes any spark of self-respect.

When a mother and daughter find mutual respect, their love blooms in a beautiful way.

Love Respects

Respect helps love bloom in four different ways:

1. It eliminates jealousy and envy
2. It prevents boasting and pride
3. It discourages haughtiness, selfishness, and rudeness
4. It opens minds to others' ideas by never demanding its own way

How does respect eliminate jealous and envy? Look at a team sport, such as football. You Monday-night-football widows will understand this simple illustration.

Let's suppose that Lynn Swann (a receiver) has just heard the play called by Terry Bradshaw (a quarterback). Suppose Terry told Lynn that he wanted him to go down and out. But Lynn doesn't like the call. He decides on his own that it would be better if he were to cut back over the middle. Well, if Lynn did that, I would bet, even with my limited knowledge of football, that that pass would be incomplete.

Lynn must respect Terry's judgment as quarterback just as Terry must respect Lynn's abilities as receiver. Terry should be aware of Lynn's weaknesses, as well as his strengths, and needs to gear his passes accordingly. That's teamwork. That's respect in action.

Terrific results come to mothers and daughters who achieve this goal, but it's not easy. Mothers and daughters are not excluded from the common sense of competition built into female relationships. Daughters wonder: *Will I be as pretty as my mother? maybe prettier? Will I be as successful? more so?* The mother asks herself: *Will my daughter be prettier than I am? more successful?*

My friends and I often compete to keep our figures in line. I can remember my mother having diet contests with her hairdresser to see who could lose the most weight.

This spirit of competition remains to be healthy and spurs us on to improve ourselves as long as we maintain respect. When respect gets lost in the competition game, jealousy and envy can easily set in. When we lose the spirit of teamwork to a spirit of selfishness and to the promotion of our own ideas no matter what the cost, the love becomes stifled.

Firsthand experience taught me what a delicate balance between competition and team spirit exists in mother-daughter relationships. Mother and I recently reexamined our feelings for each other.

I always respected my mother to some degree. My admiration soared when I began to work as her assistant. Prior to that I had only observed her abilities as a homemaker. I received only vague impressions of her expertise in other areas.

Most of my ignorance about mother's talents was due to my absorption in my own world of the church's youth department. Swamped with counseling sessions, youth activities, and Bible studies, I was blinded to everything around me. After four years of working round the clock with young people, I woke up one day, emotionally and physically exhausted. My depleted energies told me I had to move on to another vocation.

Love Respects

When I announced my plans to resign to my mother, she fervently reproved me with, "Oh, Sheila! You can't quit! You have so much to offer the ministry. It would be a terrible waste if you resigned."

Challenged by her claim concerning my value, I said, "Yeah? Well, if you think I have so much to offer, then why don't *you* hire me as your assistant."

I had only a foggy idea of what mother's job entailed, but one thing was clear: She had too much to do. In fact she was about as overworked in her department as I had been in mine.

Actually the idea of working for my mother was silly. Mother is a full-time volunteer. Whoever heard of hiring a full-time assistant for a volunteer? However, mother needed help, and I seemed the most logical person for the job. I had been raised by her. If anyone could think as she did, it would be someone who had spent a great deal of time with her. I had spent a lifetime!

That first year I quickly realized mother was far more brilliant and creative than I ever imagined. I had no idea of the immense influence she exerted on the entire Robert Schuller Ministries. I began to understand that mother was the troubleshooter for the entire organization. If anyone had a question that couldn't be answered, someone always advised, "Go ask Arvella."

That year I swelled with pride and admiration for my mother. My respect soared to new heights. She was not only a terrific mother, but also an excellent boss—both challenging and encouraging.

At first I held very limited responsibilities. I learned about the programming and editing for the "Hour of Power" from the ground floor. I merely carried out mother's orders or made suggestions when she asked for them. She made the decisions concerning which singer would perform on which Sunday, what song would be sung, and how it would be arranged. Once the show was taped, mother decided what was left in and what came out.

The first year, my influence was minimal. I gave contributions when she asked for them. But I didn't mind. I had a lot to learn. The job was complicated. Just when I thought I had it all figured out, I'd discover something else to learn. Mother was a master, and I knew it would take time to learn the job, just as it had taken her years to gain her experience.

At first I felt satisfied with my role of assistant and the fact that I didn't make the decisions. I didn't relish being in mother's shoes. I so highly respected her expertise that I never thought I could do as well.

But suddenly everything changed drastically. Carol had her accident. Everything was thrown topsy-turvy. Mother was completely tied to helping her invalid daughter. As Carol braved repeated surgery and raging infections, mother rarely left her side.

After Carol's accident, mother could not act as a church volunteer. I was the natural substitute. Although I expected new responsibilities as a result of Carol's accident, it unnerved me when mother asked, "Sheila, will you be able to take over for me? I won't

Love Respects

possibly be able to do all my work for the 'Hour of Power.' "

"Sure, mom, as long as I can call on you for advice."

Inside I shook. The job looked immense. The responsibilities seemed overwhelming. Essentially I would inherit the position of program designer for the "Hour of Power." I felt the success or failure of the program rested on my shoulders.

I met with mother whenever I could, in the hospital coffee shop or while Carol napped, but mother's mind was usually elsewhere. Many times, I left meetings with her, not having scratched the surface of my problems. I returned to my office, said a prayer, and made the decisions that kept things going.

As the months stretched into a year, I began to grow into my new role. I enjoyed the expanded creativity that came with extended responsibility. I felt more important and definitely needed.

I was not the only one that was growing stronger. So was Carol. As she did, mother had more and more time on her hands. She gradually became increasingly involved with the "Hour of Power." Before I knew it, decisions I made were no longer decisions, but mere suggestions. When I called in song selections to the music department, I'd hear that mother had called and changed my plans. I no longer held the position of boss. I lost the role I had been enjoying. It hurt.

As more and more of my suggestions were rejected I began to feel increasingly insecure. My feelings were bruised so often that I no longer respected my ability to be a valuable employee.

Mother never said to me, "I'm the boss now." It occurred as a silent evolution. Perhaps if we had discussed it as it happened, my hurt feelings might have been spared. However, I continued to bury my insecurities, until one day I couldn't bear any more. I lashed out with, "I quit!"

Mother looked stunned. "Sheila. What in the world brought this on?"

"Nothing," I murmured as tears welled up in my eyes. I turned to race out the door. Mother stopped me, turned me toward her and asked, bewildered, "What did I do to hurt you so?"

"It's just that you never seem to like my ideas anymore."

"I'm sorry. I'm only trying to help make the 'Hour of Power' the best it can be. You want that, too, don't you?"

"Yes, of course I do. It's just that—well—I'm used to being my own boss. Nobody said I was no longer in charge. It just kind of happened." As difficult as I found it to tell mother how I felt, I continued, "I'm really reluctant to tell you how I feel, because you might feel sorry for me and might purposely avoid getting involved again. I know how much you love the 'Hour of Power' and how much you love your work. I don't want to get in your way."

"I enjoy my job, that's true. But, even more, I want to work with you. I'd really be lost without you, Sheila.

Please reconsider. I think we make a pretty good team!"

"Yeah. I think so, too. Okay, mom. You've got yourself a teammate."

I put my arms around mother and said as I hugged her, "I'm sorry, mom. How rude of me to think I could do the whole job by myself!"

"Well, you *could* do a good job without me; you proved that when Carol was in the hospital. I just think we'll do a *terrific* job together."

Mom was right. Together we make a great team. We know and appreciate each other's strength and weaknesses, and put together better programs than we did when we worked by ourselves. Not only that, but the job is twice as much fun working on a team as it was working alone.

The same principles of mutual respect apply to all mothers and daughters, whether or not they work together. Those who have problems with competition, jealousy, or envy should make a real effort to develop mutual respect and a spirit of teamwork.

If a mother wants to develop team spirit, love, and respect with her daughter, she makes a conscious effort to build up her daughter. She develops sensitivity to her daughter's need for self-respect and minimizes the attention paid to her own accomplishments. Instead she centers her attention on her daughter's strengths.

Respect is never boastful or proud. Boasting and airs of arrogance accelerate competitive feelings between mothers and daughters. Self-congratulatory attitudes deepen jealousy and envy.

As for daughters, they can help develop love in this relationship by abstaining from rudeness. Unfortunately some daughters feel they can say anything they want to their mothers, no matter how rude it seems. Families may carry freedom of expression too far.

Not all disrespect is as obvious as rudeness. Haughtiness also indicates a lack of respect. This attitude shows up most often in daughters who consider themselves modern and advanced in their thinking. These young women have no patience with the life-styles of their mothers or grandmothers. In their pursuit of a better life, many daughters arrogantly toss out the values their mothers taught them, along with the "outdated" methods.

Many women view such traditional roles as housewife, homemaker, and mother as limiting, downgrading, and demeaning. Some vow that their lives will never be as mundane and meaningless as their mothers'. So they choose a career over a family, the office over home.

I do not feel that there is anything wrong with choosing a career over a family. I do object to those women who think any career is better than that of a housewife's. Those who harbor such a prejudice are guilty of haughtiness and had better consider their ignorance on the matter.

In fact, many women find the jobs in their homes very creative and meaningful. Many housewives con-

Love Respects

cur that their situation offers endless opportunities and a wide variety of endeavors.

In addition to the daughters who suffer prejudice toward their mothers' choice of careers, some daughters resent the submission and the apparent restriction that comes with marriage. They refuse to be used or dominated by a man or by children. They look out only for themselves and pursue their own identities.

In the process, many young women end up tossing out values such as service, caring, and commitment. In their search for self-development, they find loneliness. Jesus said, "Whoever wishes to save his life will lose it; but whoever loses his life for my sake will find it" (Matthew 16:25).

Some very lonely women will tell you how true that statement is. In their grand plan for their lives, they forgot to include service and giving of themselves to others. In return, no one wanted to give to them. Isolation became the natural result.

The smart daughter respects her mother as someone more experienced, and probably wiser, than she. Then she distinguishes between her mother's *values* and her *methods* and appraises them separately. She will carefully examine these values and decide which ones she can adopt. But she will be careful not to be swayed in her judgments by the methods. Rather she will choose her values and then search for her own implementation methods.

A prime example of a woman who has found new methods for her time-proven values is Elizabeth Dole. She is a graduate of Harvard Law School and an active and successful career woman. Shortly after her graduation from law school, Elizabeth served on the Federal Trade Commission. In 1981 President Reagan appointed her public liaison for the White House. In addition to being the highest ranking woman on the White House staff, she is the wife of Senator Robert Dole, from Kansas.

Elizabeth's roles and life-style are far different from her mother's and her grandmother's. At first glance these women, the White House lawyer and the ninety-nine-year-old grandma, appear to have little in common. But when you look closely, you see their values are the same. Elizabeth learned to serve others by watching her grandmother in action. Every Sunday the older woman held Bible studies in her home, for the neighborhood children, including Elizabeth. Every cent she could spare was given to missionaries or ministers, to help tell people about her Lord.

Elizabeth carefully appraised her grandmother's values and decided to make them her own. Like her grandmother, Elizabeth made Jesus the center of her life. Though her life-style is vastly different from her grandmother's, Elizabeth shares the same goals. Both have lived and still do live each day to help others and to serve Jesus any way they can. From her grandmother, Elizabeth learned to waken each morning and look to see what God had in mind for the new day. To help her accomplish all she feels God wants her to, Elizabeth keeps her grandmother's favorite Bible verse on her desk in the White House: "Trust in the Lord

Love Respects

with all thine heart and lean not unto thine own understanding" (Proverbs 3:5).

Respect does not show itself in a haughty or rude attitude. Daughters like Elizabeth, who respect their mothers and their grandmothers, have the best outlook on life. They are the winners. These women lead fulfilled lives because they will always find love and appreciation. Their respect for others encourages others to respect them.

Ultimately every woman searches for respect. The Women's Liberation Movement arose, not because women felt unloved or unappreciated, but because they felt unrespected. Women today need to be respected by men, by other women, and by themselves.

Unfortunately many go about trying to get respect in the wrong way. In their pursuit, many women aggressively present their ideas and their personhood, but fail to maintain respect for others. In so doing, they become guilty of the very thing they accuse others of: disrespect. Too often, through harsh assertiveness, women miss the goal they aim for. Rather than earning respect, they earn fear.

If a mother or daughter wants to be respected, she will learn to respect. She will not seek to have *her* way, but will seek the *right* way. Respect does not demand its own way. It pursues the best way. My father has said, "I would rather do it right and succeed than do it my way and fail."

I learned how right he is. Like other women, I have worked on a professional basis with men who have fought my involvement, sneared at my ideas, and—worst of all—patronized me. But I have also worked with men who have respected me and have not been afraid to show it.

Ironically the men with the most degrees and the most credentials have treated me with the most respect. For example, take Michael Kidd, a television director I worked with for one season. I felt scared to death when they told me I would be working with him, for his list of movie credits and Tony Awards is endless.

Yet I soon discovered that Michael is very sure of himself and his ideas. Secure in his own self-worth, he feels free to consider everyone's ideas, even the script girls'. He never demands his own way. He doesn't have to. Rather he seeks the best way. The result? Michael became one of the most successful and beloved men in all Broadway and Hollywood.

Where can mothers find this same kind of respect for themselves and others? from the source of love, and from the source of respect: God.

God loves us. He wants to help us respect ourselves and love ourselves as much as *He* loves and respects us.

Many find it difficult to realize that God loves them. Even a great king had trouble feeling worthy of God's attention, much less His love and respect. He wrote: "Who am I that you [God] are mindful of me? Who am I that you visit with me? For you have made me a little lower than the angels and have crowned me with glory and honor" (Psalms 8:5).

Love Respects

Whoever this king was, he must have been a truly great person to have commanded God's attention and concern. He must have ruled a powerful empire for God to make the effort to go talk to him personally. He must surely have been a kind and benevolent monarch for God to bring crowns and heap glory and honor on him. Here is the kind of man who would demand the respect of a nation—indeed, the world.

Who was he? the great King David. His words are not those of a king, but of a man. He speaks not only for himself, but for you and me.

Whom does God visit and crown with glory and honor? you and me. Mothers and daughters alike, all are important to God. The ruler of the universe loves and respects us and wants to crown our relationships with glory and honor. Once we know and feel God's love, relationships will be healed, and the love that can exist between mothers and daughters will be revealed.

10

Love Reflects

"Mirror, mirror, on the wall, who's the fairest of them all?" So asked the beautiful queen of her magic mirror. Indeed, all mirrors are almost magical. You can look into a piece of silvered glass and see what you really look like. Or can you? If the mirror is clean and polished, then, yes, you can get an honest reflection. But if you look in a blurred mirror, or a distorted funhouse one, then you'll see a wide assortment of inaccurate reflections. The mirror image is as dependent on the shape and cleanliness of the surface as it is on the item being reflected.

This sort of joint dependence can be seen in mother-daughter relationships. Mothers, like mirrors, reflect back to their daughters who they are and whom they can become. Obviously what the mother reflects depends on what kind of woman the daughter has become. However the mother can choose to reflect a clear image of the woman her daughter is, or she can choose to alter the reflection.

Let me illustrate: If a daughter has on a dress that is all wrong for her, her mother can reflect her opinions honestly and clearly; or she can distort the picture and

Love Reflects

say, "That looks beautiful on you, honey," when in fact it doesn't.

Or suppose an otherwise successful daughter has a problem with selfishness. The mother can reflect an image of perfection, blurring the selfishness, never bringing it to her daughter's attention; or she can reflect a totally honest picture: selfishness and all.

The choice is not always easy. No one wants to reflect imperfections, weaknesses, or ugliness. No one wants to be the bearer of bad news. Yet mother as well as daughter will have to choose what to reflect to a loved one. She has to deal with that person's weaknesses and will have to decide what to do with her observations.

Will your reflection be honest? Do you base it on love? Consider the best course for the one you care about: honest exposure or discrete silence? Can a mother reflect painful truths to her daughter in such a way as to build her up rather than hurt her? Can she simultaneously maintain loyalty to her daughter's feelings and loyalty to integrity?

If we look to 1 Corinthians 13, we find our answer. In the last verse of our love passage we read: "When you love someone you will be loyal to him [or her] no matter what the cost."

Loyalty is the key word. When you think about it, loyalty by its very nature implies honesty. If you carefully look at any large corporation, you'll see what I mean. A large-corporation president has many people working for him. Of these, probably only a handful would be real, true-blue loyal employees. They love the company and the president enough to be honest with him. The other yes-men care only about themselves and so only tell the president what he wants to hear.

Loyalty and honesty are essential to any love relationship. *Constructive* honesty, rooted in love, can nobly reflect the mother-daughter relationship.

I have emphasized the word *constructive* and thereby have chosen to qualify the term *honesty*. I believe various degrees of honesty exist, ranging from the constructive to the destructive. We may "speak the truth" and hurt people in the process. Not all honesty is valuable, and not all words of truth are rooted in love.

Constructive honesty builds up, but destructive honesty tears down. One looks for solutions, but the other points out weak spots. One hurts, but the other heals.

Speaking the truth in love so that it heals, builds up, and restores is not an easy task. Many have failed, including my mother and me. There have been times when mom and I have not been as sensitive as we could have been. But for all the times my feelings have gotten bruised, they have never been as battered as they were by my brother, Bob.

When I was in high school, Bob, in junior high school, heard me crying in my bedroom.

"Hey, Sheila—Shoe [his pet name for me]—how come you're crying?"

"Leave me alone!"

Love Reflects

"Aw, come on; what's wrong?"

On a sudden impulse I decided to tell him what was bugging me. "Well, I never get asked out on a date. Bob, you're a boy; tell me what's wrong with me?"

"You really want to know?"

"Yeah!"

"You're fat!"

My trickle of tears suddenly burst into a raging torrent. I threw myself on my bed and screamed at him, "Get out! I don't ever want to speak to you again!"

Mom came running in, "What in the world is going on in here?"

"It's Bob! He's so mean. He said that I was—fat!" I threw myself across my bed again.

Bob quickly defended himself with, "She asked me, mom. I just told her the truth."

Truth? If that was the truth, I didn't want to have anything to do with it! But it was true: I was fat. I knew I needed to lose weight, but I didn't need to hear it from my kid brother. And hearing it from Bob only made me cry harder and made me feel more insecure, which only resulted in more eating binges and more excess weight. Bob's honesty acted destructively. He pointed out my weak spot and made it weaker with one swift sentence, "You're fat!"

I really don't blame Bob. It was as much my fault as his. First of all, I had no reason to think that my brother, who was known for teasing, would give me a gentle answer, which is *really* what I wanted. Actually I'd have to admit that I really didn't *want* Bob to be honest with me. I really wanted him to say, "Sheila, I don't have any idea why the boys don't ask you out. I think you're positively beautiful."

Of course my young brother was by no means mature enough to read between the lines. He heard my question for what it was and gave an honest answer.

Few people master the art of constructive honesty, much less junior-high-school-age brothers. Discovering the ability to convey truth without hurting is a delicate operation. Fortunately for me, my mother constructively used her more mature and adept ability for reflecting honesty.

Even though I knew I was overweight and even though my brother told me I was fat, I didn't really do anything about it. I maintained my extra weight throughout high school and brought the pounds with me to college. There, thanks to late-night snacks of popcorn, pizza, and sundaes, I added twenty more.

Somehow I managed to look in the mirror every day without seeing the pounds go on. I don't know if the mirrors at college were only big enough to reflect anyone from the shoulders up, if I developed an elongated astigmatism in my eyesight, or what. But however I did it, I managed to twist the image in the mirror to see what I wanted to see. I didn't see a fat or obese person, just a chubby one. I believed I was built big—heavy bones, and so on—and I was just meant to go through life as a big person. Oh, it often occurred to me that I should lose a few pounds: maybe five or ten. But I never thought I needed to lose twenty-five! No, that much fat was not reflected in my mirror.

But mom saw all the weight and the depression that

Love Reflects

I tried to deny to everyone, including myself. Where I saw a big girl who only needed to lose a few pounds, mother saw a girl whose life was "waisting" away. Where I saw a girl who would always be big, my mother saw a girl who had the potential for being slim and beautiful. My images of myself were distorted. Mom saw the truth. But how could she reflect it in such a way that I would be helped and not hurt?

She waited until I graduated from college and returned home. Then she carefully spoke to me. "Sheila, you're a beautiful girl. Do you know that if you lost about twenty pounds, you'd be a knockout?"

I felt stunned. Me, a knockout? the kind of girl whom guys would notice walking down the street? I *never* thought of myself that way. But mother did. If she thought I could be that beautiful, maybe I could be.

Suddenly I imagined myself twenty pounds lighter. The image of myself at that new weight was far more beautiful. I liked what I saw and decided then and there that I'd do it. And I did.

The image transplant mother performed with that one simple, concise sentence did it for me. How? What made her honesty constructive and not destructive? Mother reflected an honest picture of what I could be. Not what I was, but what I could be!

She said nothing to reinforce the already negative image I had of myself. She didn't say I was unattractive at that weight, because she didn't have to; I already knew that.

Rather, her words were positive: "Sheila, you're a

beautiful girl. You could be a knockout if you lost about twenty pounds." Through her words of love, she reflected the image of the woman I could be.

Honest reflections don't have to be of images as they are *now*. They can be projections of possibilities and opportunities, without losing integrity.

What the mirror reflects is only half the relationship. The other half lies in the eyes of the beholder, in how she accepts and interprets the reflection.

Often mirror images are misinterpreted. We all ask the mirror on the wall, "How do I look?" Yet we may only see images tainted by our inner feelings. If we feel insecure, then we see more fat, more pimples, more wrinkles than are really there. Or if we attempt to justify ourselves, we can see just the opposite. When I was overweight, I saw myself as thinner than I really was and promptly thought, *Great! Now I can go out and have a hot-fudge sundae!*

So we daughters may interpret or *mis*interpret what our mothers try to tell us in love. We need their honest appraisal and should welcome it.

It's valuable to be able to go to someone whom you know loves you and will be honest with you: A magic mirror who will tell you honestly and lovingly how you look and how you're doing.

How Do I Look?

Mom and I frequently ask each other, "How do I look?" We trust each other to give good, honest appraisals of our clothes, our makeup, hairstyles, and so on. Every woman cares about her appearance. It forms a vital part of her sense of self-esteem. The woman who feels good about herself is free to do her job in life, whether it be as a mother and a wife, a single or career woman.

Like all women, the way we feel about ourselves depends on how we think we look. The better we look and the better we think we look, the better we feel.

This is not just vanity. Society dictates that the more beautiful a woman looks, the greater her worth as a human being. We have all read the poem that describes little girls as "sugar and spice and everything nice" and noticed the cute accompanying drawings of sweet, pretty girls.

Every little girl has sat on her mother's knee and heard the story of Cinderella and her *tiny* glass slipper. Heaven help those of us who wear size-ten shoes! Will the handsome prince want us? And what young woman hasn't wondered, *Am I a sleeping beauty? When, oh, when will my beauty wake up?*

Dr. James Dobson substantiates the importance society places on beauty as a measure of a person's worth in his valuable book *Hide or Seek*. Beauty, he states, rates first in the worth of an individual as he or she is judged by others; the second rating concerns intelligence and special abilities, as in music or sports. How true! How terribly unfair! Yet we mothers can not entirely shelter our daughters from this judgment. The media bombards them with the philosophy that they must be beautiful in order to be worthwhile. Television and magazines flaunt beauty as a woman's most prized possession.

Mothers who try to ignore this fact will not be as helpful to their daughters as those who realize that all females are evaluated by their looks as well as their abilities—as much by themselves as by anyone. We cannot change the way the whole world thinks, but we can help our daughters look their very best. We can also teach them to look beyond, to the true values in life: their inner beauties.

How Am I Doing?

Since mom is my magic mirror, I often ask her, "Mirror, mirror, on the wall, am I fair?" I want to know if I look okay. Mother often asks me the same question. Another question that we frequently ask each other is, "How do I fare?" Or, "How am I doing?" I frequently ask this question of mother, especially now that I am a new mother. I face so much confusion concerning child-rearing philosophies that I often doubt my abilities as a mother. After reading all the how-to books on raising babies, I easily judge myself too harshly. I never seem to meet up with the standards the so-called experts recommend for healthy child development.

Of course no one meets them, but the problem comes when I focus my attention on all my imperfections. Then my maternal successes become overshadowed by my failures, until I feel discouraged and despondent.

I have learned that I stand too close to myself to see myself accurately. My self-examination mirror is often distorted. Just as I look at myself in the mirror and see

Love Reflects

myself as fatter or thinner than I really am, so when I look at myself as a mother, I often see a false image.

That's where mother has proved extremely valuable. I often call and describe the feelings that plague me. I share fears and worries about my inadequacies as a young mother, as a wife, or even as her assistant. I trust her honest appraisal. Sometimes she says, "Yes, Sheila, I think you need to work on this area of your life. But then most women do; why, I remember feeling the very way you do."

Or she says, "Oh, Sheila. You're being far too hard on yourself. You really are a much better mother than you give yourself credit for."

Over the years I have found tremendous freedom in being able to share my weaknesses with mother. Often, overcome with feelings of guilt and remorse, I find, after sharing them with mother, that I am normal. Comfort comes with the discovery that many women share my fears and worries. At those times, mother reflects unconditional love and constructive honesty.

Mothers mirror their daughters, but daughters also mirror their mothers. Mother also asks me, "How am I doing?" Whenever she speaks or addresses a meeting, she asks me, "How did I do?" I answer her honestly, but I try to be constructive. I first tell her what I liked. Then if I noticed something she could have said or done to improve her presentation, I tell her. But I have a policy: I never point out a weakness until I can suggest a solution.

Why do we bother to inquire how we're doing? because we care about each other and want our lives to reflect excellence. Neither mother nor I want to be *the* best, but we do want to be *our* best. Has my mother been the best mother she could be? Has she been successful? I reflect the answer in the woman and mother I am. As a successful mother, wife, and young woman, I reflect and reassure mother of her own success as a mother. As I grow and mature into a productive, fulfilled, and happy individual, I reflect to all I meet that my mother has done a good job. When mom looks at me, I reflect the answer to the question "Have I been successful as a mother?"

Of course, I'm not perfect, and neither is mom. She sometimes sees attributes mirrored that she may not want repeated in my younger brothers and sisters. Conversely she may see attributes in me that she wishes she'd emphasized more in them.

The fact that I have chosen to be a mother reflects the fact that my mother has been successful. I realized this last year at the mother-daughter banquet at our church. My mother and I gave the closing comments to the hundreds of women gathered there. I was eight months pregnant at the time. As I stood by mom at the podium, she said, "The greatest compliment a daughter pays her mother is choosing motherhood herself." It's true! My mother paid tribute to my grandmother when she decided to have me. I in turn paid tribute to her when I decided to have Jason.

We enjoy receiving honest compliments such as these. Truthful appraisals are not as easy to accept, however, if they point out a weak spot. But if the truth

Love Reflects

can be said in love and if your critic shows an attitude of searching for a solution, then honest evaluation between a mother and a daughter can be the highest expression of love.

"Mirror, mirror, on the wall, who's the fairest of them all?" the wicked queen asked her magic mirror. She intended to hurt and destroy Snow White.

We mothers and daughters, unlike the wicked queen and Snow White, can reflect love, constructive honesty, and loyalty. We can ask each other, "Are we fair?" "How do we fare?"

Our answers can help and heal and restore if we remember to reflect not necessarily what is, but *what can be*. Never has the power of this principle been more forcefully illustrated than in the musical drama, "The Man of La Mancha."

Here we meet a man: Don Quixote of La Mancha. Some say he is crazy. But he believes that "others see life as it is; I see it as it can become." When he looks at a broken-down old swayback, he sees a noble steed. When he looks in the mirror, he sees not a round-shouldered old man, but a knight-errant. His bent, rusting sword is as strong and gleaming as Excalibur. And his journey through the countryside of Spain is a glorious quest. A quest—ah, that means a search for something that is lost.

Only a few days into this quest, Don Quixote's path crosses that of a woman—a prostitute. But as he does with everything else, he sees her not as she is, but as she can become. He sees her not as a prostitute, but as a *lady*. He gallantly rides up to her and calls out,

"My lady!" Aldonza looks around, bewildered, and seeing no one else in sight, sneers, "Who me?"

"Yes, you! I am a knight-errant! Every knight needs a lady, and you shall be my lady. You shall be my Dulcinea, which means, 'my sweetness.' "

"Dulcinea? Hah! My name is Aldonza! You want to know what I really am? I was born in a ditch by a mother who left me there naked and cold and too hungry to cry. I never blamed her, I'm sure she left hoping that I'd have the good sense to die! Dulcinea? No! I'm only Aldonza—the whore!" With that, she storms off the stage.

The play progresses as the man of La Mancha pursues his quest. But nobody believes him. Nobody sees the good in life that he sees. Finally, he lies on his deathbed, dying of a broken heart.

Suddenly, a beautiful Spanish woman enters. She is dressed in a lovely gown, with a lacy mantilla gracefully crowning her head. This lady glides over to the dying man of La Mancha and cries out, "My lord! My lord!"

The old man looks up and whispers, "Who—who are you?"

"Do you not remember me? Oh, you must remember. You called me 'your lady,' 'your Dulcinea.' Remember you taught me to dream impossible dreams and reach for the highest stars? You helped me to see the me that could be."

The man of La Mancha replies gustily, "Yes! Yes! I remember. You are my Dulcinea. You are my lady!"

He saw her not as she was, but as she could or, in-

Love Reflects

deed, did become. This is love at its best. This is the love Jesus wants in us. He sees us not as we are but as we can become. The love Christ reflects is healing and constructive. Though Christ was scorned and bears the scars, He strives with His last ounce of courage to reach the impossible stars—that's you and me—with his love.

"If you love someone, you will be loyal to him no matter what the cost." Jesus paid the cost of His loyalty to us: death on a cross. He only asks in return that we love others as best we can and that we reflect His love as clearly and beautifully as possible.

11

The Supreme Model of Love

Every mother can be a star. Every mother and daughter can discover freedom, friendship, and love in their relationship, *if* they can learn to share one more thing: faith. The mother who chooses to believe in herself, in her daughter, and in God will be a queen.

Successful mothers have chosen belief over doubt, faith over fear. They know what they believe and whom they believe in.

All mothers model faith or faithlessness. There is no middle ground. No one avoids the choice, for not choosing between belief and unbelief means a choice of doubt. Whether or not we like it, mothers will model either belief or unbelief, trust or skepticism, doubt or faith.

The choice is actually twofold: We must choose whether or not to believe; we must choose what or whom we believe in. Ironically, the way we answer the first question depends on how we answer the second. You cannot believe unless you have something or someone to believe in.

Successful mothers have an ideal model in whom they believe and after whom they pattern their lives. These star mothers make it a priority in their lives to know their Ideal Model intimately and personally.

When we take a close look at the life of Naomi, related to us in the Bible, in the Book of Ruth, we can see this principle come into play. Naomi was a star mother-in-law. Her Ideal One was God. Following Him was the most important thing in her life. Nothing deterred her from her steadfast pursuit of His will for her life. Despite the numerous trials she encountered, she modeled faith to all who knew her.

Naomi was a Jew. She was born and raised in Bethlehem and brought up in the Judaic faith. There she became the wife of Elimelech, who shared her religious heritage. These newlyweds were very happy in their beloved land, until the great famine struck. Forced to search for food, Naomi and Elimelech found refuge in the neighboring land of Moab. There they built new lives for themselves and their two sons.

Though far from their home and alone in a heathen land, the couple continued to believe in God and raised their sons in the Judaic faith.

When the boys grew to be young men and reached marriageable age, they each took a Moabite wife, one of whom was named Ruth. The whole family lived together happily for ten years. Ruth and her sister-in-law came to love their husbands as well as their mother- and father-in-law, Naomi and Elimelech.

Then tragedy struck, all three men died, and the women were left widowed. Naomi felt grief stricken. Stripped of her husband and sons, she decided to return to her home. When she announced her intention to leave, Ruth pleaded with her to take her along.

The Supreme Model of Love

Naomi replied, "No, return to your mother's house. May the Lord deal kindly with you as you have dealt with me."

Naomi must have been a wonderful mother-in-law. She must have modeled a remarkable faith and a beautiful love, for Ruth insisted on following her. She said, "Entreat me not to leave you or to return from following you; for where you go I will go, and where you lodge I will lodge; your people shall be my people, and your God my God" (Ruth 1:16 RSV).

Ruth apparently loved and trusted Naomi a great deal, for she chose to follow her even to unknown lands and strange peoples. We can also assume that Naomi modeled a beautiful faith, for Ruth wanted to believe in the same God Naomi believed in. She wanted to share Naomi's faith.

Ruth's encounter with Naomi's God of love must have been a stark contrast to her experience with the Moabite religion, which was steeped in fear of gods who sought to destroy. How wonderful for Ruth, after coming out of such a fear-filled tradition, to discover Naomi's God of love.

When Ruth found a God she could love and trust, she easily believed in him. Naturally she wanted to follow a woman who modeled such a loving faith.

Ruth's decision proved wise. When she followed Naomi, she left behind fear and unbelief and went on to find love and trust. In Bethlehem Ruth found love with a man named Boaz. How they met and married became one of the most beloved love stories of all time.

Boaz was a kinsman of Elimelech and a man of

wealth. Ruth went to his barley field to glean among the ears of grain, after the reapers had passed through. Customarily in those times poor people followed the reapers to gather any grains they had left behind. This harvest was theirs to keep.

One evening, after Ruth had gleaned all day, gathering food for herself and for Naomi, Boaz came from Bethlehem. He noticed Ruth immediately. She was a stranger, so he asked his servant who was in charge of the reapers, "Whose maiden is this?" The servant replied, ". . . It is the Moabite maiden, who came back with Naomi from the country of Moab. She said, 'Pray, let me glean and gather among the sheaves after the reapers.' So she came, and she has continued from early morning until now, without resting even for a moment."

Boaz was touched by this woman who displayed such love and devotion to his kinsman, Naomi. He said to Ruth, ". . . Now listen, my daughter, do not go to glean in another field or leave this one, but keep close to my maidens. Let your eyes be upon the field which they are reaping, and go after them. Have I not charged the young men not to molest you? And when you are thirsty, go to the vessels and drink what the young men have drawn."

Ruth fell on her face, bowing to the ground, and said to him. "Why have I found favor in your eyes that you should take notice of me, when I am a foreigner?"

Boaz answered her, "All that you have done for your mother-in-law since the death of your husband has been fully told me, and how you left your father and mother and your native land and came to a people that you did not know before. The Lord recompense you for what you have done, and a full reward be given you by the Lord, the God of Israel, under whose wings you have come to take refuge!" (Ruth 2:5–12 RSV).

The God of Israel did repay her for trusting in him. He brought love into her life, through Boaz. They married and brought forth sons, one of whom was the forebear of Jesus.

The God Ruth chose to follow and believe in is a God who strengthens and heals, who takes hurts and turns them into beauty. From a childless widow, He brought forth sons, one of whom would be the greatest of all: Jesus Christ. God brought love into Ruth's life through Naomi and Boaz and the ultimate love into the world through Jesus Christ.

When Naomi gave Ruth the gift of faith, she gave the gift of love to the world. Therefore, she is a star of mothers. The God these women believed in is a loving God, the source of love, who teaches all mothers everywhere how to love. He also cares. He clothes the lilies and feeds the sparrows. He numbers the hairs on our heads. Surely, He can take care of all our needs, and we can count on Him to help us and provide for us in time of trouble.

Arleta Richardson, in her book *In Grandma's Attic,* shares how her grandmother modeled faith in a God who cares. This grandmother, who was a firm believer in prayer, taught little Arleta that God always answers prayers when they are prayed in faith. But she always carefully added that she never asked God for anything she could provide for herself.

The following incident clearly illustrates the faith this grandma had in a God who cared for her and her loved ones.

One day, while sitting in the little country church, she listened to her husband, the preacher, giving his Sunday sermon. Suddenly, she noticed his toes peeking out from his well-worn shoes. *Oh, my,* she thought, *This will never do. I can't possibly let Len stand up there and preach with his toes showing.* But she knew there was no money for new shoes. She knew that if Len was going to get new shoes, the Lord would have to provide them. So Arleta's grandma and grandpa got down on their knees and asked God to send them a pair of shoes.

One week later, just one day before grandpa was scheduled to preach again, a neighbor drove up in his buggy. He stopped to chat a while, and in the course of the conversation he mentioned that he had a pair of shoes that didn't fit right. So he said, "Len, would you like to have them?"

Grandpa beamed and said, "Yes, sir, I would!"

The visitor asked, "How do you know? You haven't tried them on yet."

Len quietly said, "I'm not worried about that. When the Lord sends shoes, He sends the right size!"

Arleta's grandparents modeled faith in a God who cares and who's interested in the details—even shoe sizes! Through her life and her words Arleta's

The Supreme Model of Love

grandma taught her that you can always trust and believe in God.

That grandmother modeled her faith for her children and her children's children. She knew who her God was. Do you? Do I? Do you have faith to give your daughter? Have you given her the gift of believing—in herself and in her dreams?

Many mothers have taught their daughters to believe but have not taught them whom to believe in. Such faith is weak and shallow, for faith can only be as strong as the object on which it focuses.

The anchor is only as solid as the rock to which it is grounded. This is also true of faith. Faith strong enough to weather trials must be based in a powerful, loving, and caring God. He alone carrys us through the really dark times. I know this by experience.

Like Ruth and Arleta, I chose to follow the faith of my mother and my mother's mother. I adopted their belief in a strong, loving, caring, and forgiving God. I was a young girl when I decided to let God have control of my life. In so doing, I threw down my anchor of faith and secured it on the rock of God's power and grace.

I cast my anchor out and firmly rooted it on a rock. But how strong was this rock? Would it hold if a storm came? Would my faith carry me through a crisis?

I found out when the storm hit, and it was a hurricane—when Carol was hurt and maimed for life. The shock of the news and the pain it brought tested my faith and the strength of my God. Wave after wave of anguish beat against me. The storm was a biggie, but

God was bigger. Down below the churning waters, my anchor held onto a boulder that never budged.

Throughout the ordeal, I never doubted God's love for Carol. I completely trusted His sovereignty and His plan for Carol, which I believed would be for her good. Carol also completely trusted God's love and care for her. Even as she lay in the ditch, waiting for the ambulance to come, with leg severed and an acute loss of blood, she prayed over and over again, "When I walk through the valley of the shadow of death, I will fear no evil, for thou art with me."

The gift of faith that mother and dad gave to Carol carried her through a life-threatening situation. Later it helped carry her through days of embarrassment brought on by an unsightly limb. Carol claims that the greatest gift mother ever gave her was the gift of faith.

Every mother gives her daughter gifts: clothes, jewelry, and so on. But have you given your daughter the most important gift of all: the gift of faith? If your daughter came to you today and said, "Your God shall be my God," could you give her sufficient faith? Who would your God be? Would He be a loving God? Would He be a caring God? Would He be a personal God?

"Who is your God?" is the most important question anyone ever answers. In my opinion, the star mothers all share the same answer: Jesus Christ. The star mothers all have Jesus as the center of their lives and have modeled themselves after Him. He is God incarnate, the Supreme Model of Love. Through Him and His example, mothers and daughters learn to accept

The Supreme Model of Love

each other, respect each other, and love each other. Through Him we see reflected the mothers we were created to be. He picks us up when we stumble, helps us to forgive ourselves, and gives us the courage to try again. Through Him we obtain the grace to be stars.

The key to beautiful and successful mother-daughter relationships is Jesus, and we must model our lives after His. But before we can pattern our lives after Him, we have to know who He *was*, and who He *is*.

We can easily see who Jesus *was* according to the recorded testimonies of His friends and disciples in the Bible's New Testament. We see who Jesus *is* when we examine the lives of people living today, who know Him personally.

Let me share with you the Jesus who *was*, as I know Him through my favorite Bible passages, as well as the Jesus who *is*, whom I see in my mother.

Jesus Loves the Little Children

One of the things mom and I love most about Jesus is his love for children. This bachelor, whose brilliant teachings were sought after by thousands of adults, treated children so tenderly and respectfully. On one occasion when men and women who wanted to hear him teach thronged around Jesus, a noisy group of children pushed their way up to where He sat. The disciples naturally tried to shoo them away, but Jesus stopped them and said, "Suffer the little children to come unto me, for of such is the kingdom of heaven." With that He gathered them in His arms and included them in His love.

Anyone can understand love. You don't have to be a certain age or have a special mentality to know that Jesus loves you. Jesus made that very clear when He gathered the children to Himself.

It is never too early to teach our daughters about Jesus and His love. Seeds of faith can be planted in our daughters when they are still infants.

My own mother taught me about Jesus when I was a little girl. I cannot remember a day when my mother neglected to tell me about Jesus. As early as I can remember, I heard about Him and the love and the healing that He gave to others.

Jesus Heals the Deepest Hurts

It always amazed me when I heard the stories about Jesus healing people. He made thousands of them whole. He healed lepers and blind men. He healed the deaf and the lame. The many kinds of diseases He healed were impossible to keep track of.

Jesus still heals today. He heals physical affirmities; He heals broken hearts; He heals wounded spirits and wrecked relationships.

I have never been healed of a physical problem, but I have felt Jesus heal my heart on many occasions. I have felt discouraged and heartbroken, only to have Jesus mend me with His healing touch.

I shall never forget the night I lay in bed, trying to go to sleep, but over and over again I relived the nightmare I experienced that day.

Every time I closed my eyes, I'd see John again. He was the man I loved and wanted to marry. He had said

The Supreme Model of Love

he wanted to spend his life with me. But he lied.

Who was that girl I saw him with? Why did he date others behind my back? How could he betray me and humiliate me so? I asked myself.

I turned my face to the wall and let the warm tears run down my cheek, until my pillow was wet.

Then I heard the door open. I saw my mother in the doorway. She was a shadow lit by the light that filtered in behind her. I could not see her face, but I knew that she was worried about me. She had immediately known something was wrong. She saw it on my face the moment I came home. She knew how much I loved John, and she shared my pain when I told her that the relationship was over.

She silently came over to the bed: I pretended to sleep. As far as I was concerned, she could say nothing to make me feel better. Without a word, mom bent over me and began to stroke my cheek. Lovingly she caressed me; and as her fingers softly wiped away my tears, I felt my hurt melt away. Peace flowed in. My heart was healed.

Through my mother's loving touch, Jesus healed me and gave me the courage to love again. I have seen Him do it over and over. Without so much as a word, He binds up illness and broken spirits with a single healing stroke.

Jesus Disciplines Those He Loves

Because Jesus was such a wonderful healer and teacher, multitudes of people flocked to Him. But He chose only twelve to disciple. Jesus decided to invest his energies in twelve, who could in turn train twelve, and so on, until thousands could know Him intimately.

One ingredient Jesus included in his training plan for His disciples was discipline. Discipline is a natural part of the process of discipleship.

We mothers can take a lesson in discipline from Jesus. If Jesus, the source of love, disciplined His disciples, we mothers should certainly care enough to do as much for our daughters. Jesus disciplined because he loved.

These unruly disciples certainly need as much discipline as love. One incident comes immediately to mind. The disciples and Jesus were taking a leisurely cruise across the Sea of Galilee after fulfilling a hectic schedule. Jesus was exhausted. He was human, and people had demanded a great deal of Him. So once in the privacy of a boat, out in the middle of the sea, He lay down for a much needed rest.

But the Sea of Galilee is known for sudden storms that arise from nowhere, trapping boats in the middle of its water with waves that can capsize and kill. Jesus had barely fallen asleep when one of the sudden storms hit. The waves pounded the boat furiously, and the disciples felt sure they were all doomed. They clung to the sides of the vessel; suddenly they realized that Jesus was sleeping while they were dying! One rushed over to Jesus and shook Him awake, crying, "Master, Master, do you not care that we are perishing?"

Jesus awoke, looked around Him, and said, "O ye of

The Supreme Model of Love

little faith." Then He stretched out His arms, and the winds subsided, and the waves ceased. Peace and quiet reigned.

I'm afraid I have too often been like the disciples. Sure my faith stood up in the big storm of Carol's accident; but often everyday pressures of life, the endless pile of diapers, the unending stack of dishes, and the dust that came back week after week, all piled upon me until I felt I was drowning.

One day I remember kneeling by my bed and praying, "Lord, please help me. I am drowning in my list of things to do."

I opened the Bible to this very passage. I read the verse in which the disciples were crying out, "Lord, do you not care that we are drowning?" I said, "Lord, that's just how I feel! I feel just like those disciples." He said, "Read on." I did. I saw how He stretched out His arms and said, "Peace, be still." I felt Jesus gently discipline me and say, "Sheila, have faith. Believe in Me. I will see you through. Peace, be still." His peace flowed through me. I arose from my prayer a better disciple of Jesus and a better model of His strength for my husband and my son.

I firmly believe that mothers today need to discipline their lives. If they want to model their lives after Jesus and be His disciples, they have to make time every day to get to know Jesus better. They need to get in tune with His love, His peace, and His strength.

It amazes me how much I can get out of five minutes a day reading my Bible and praying to my Lord. Sure, I toss up a lot of little prayers throughout the day, but I seem to need one special time each day, when I stop everything I'm doing and praise and thank God for what He's done for me.

It is not easy being a mother. Sometimes life becomes difficult. But if we can learn to discipline ourselves to trust in Jesus and His care and to spend time with Him every day, then we will find shade in the heat and shelter in the storm.

The poet Edna St. Vincent Millay says it so beautifully in her poem, "Jesus to His Disciples":

> I have instructed you to follow me
> What way I go;
> The road is hard and stony, as I know;
> Uphill it climbs, and from the crushing heat
> No shelter will be found
> Save in my shadow: Wherefore follow me;
>   the footprints of my feet
> Will be distinct and clear;
> However trodden on, they will not disappear.
> And see ye not at last
> How tall I am?—Even at noon I cast
> A shadow like a forest far behind me on the
>   ground.

Oh, but that we all could follow in His steps and rest in His shadow. Oh, but that we could know Him intimately and thereby model our lives after Him.

It is the aim of my mother and me to live our lives in such a way that when others look they do not see mother or me, but Jesus. All mothers can strive for that ultimate goal: to be like Jesus.

None of us will make it all the way. All of us blow it

The Supreme Model of Love

now and then. That is when we need to focus on the final, but in my opinion the most important, gift Jesus gives: redemption.

Jesus Redeems the Biggest Mistakes

Jesus never takes a mistake and throws it away; He redeems it. He takes broken people and relationships that are in a mess and transforms them into beautiful, loving mothers and daughters. Jesus can take our moments of impatience, rudeness, and selfishness, and He can redeem them and restore our love.

He is like the master weaver whose students felt no fear when undertaking new and difficult projects. When they were asked what happened when they made a mistake, they replied, "We do not cut it out. We simply show it to our teacher. He is such a skilled weaver that he can weave around our mistakes, incorporating them into the design, so that the mistake *adds* to the beauty of the finished project."

Jesus does this with our lives. He redeems our mistakes and weaves around them, incorporating them into the design of our lives, making us all the more beautiful when He is finished. He forgives us for the times when we have not been loving mothers and daughters. And He takes all the rough spots of our relationships and smoothes over them, until we are all He wants us to be.

Ruth Carter Stapleton, the sister of former President Carter, tells how Jesus redeemed her imperfect love for her daughter. As a young mother, she experienced the same apprehensions for her children that all mothers have. Ruth let her fears get the best of her. She was so afraid for her daughter that she never gave her daughter the freedom to grow and develop into a healthy, independent little girl. In the process, her daughter pushed her own identity deep within herself and stifled the urges to develop herself as a separate entity.

As a result, when it came time for her to enter kindergarten, the child became so violently ill that a physician had to be contacted. The doctor's diagnosis came as a total shock to Ruth: "Your daughter is not physically ill. She is mentally ill. You have smothered your daughter, Ruth. I suggest you set up an appointment for her to see a psychologist. Here's his number."

Ruth was devastated. Can any of us imagine a more pronounced judgment of failure as a mother? As hurt as she was, she called the doctor and set up an appointment. His schedule was full, and he could not see the child for two months, but she made the appointment anyway and waited.

Every night for the next two months, before she went to bed, Ruth went into her daughter's room. There she'd place her hand on the head of her sleeping child and pray, "Forgive me, Lord. Heal my daughter. Fill in the gaps where my loving has been less than it should have been. Smooth out the errors I made in my judgments. Show me how to love as You do."

When the two months were up, Ruth took her five-year-old daughter to the psychologist. He examined her and talked with her. He turned to Ruth and said,

The Supreme Model of Love 157

"There is nothing wrong with this child. She's just fine."

Jesus healed her daughter and redeemed Ruth's mistake. Isn't it wonderful to know that Jesus can redeem any mistake and can turn the worst errors into the most beautiful blessings? It's true, you know. There is nothing you or I could do as mothers that cannot be redeemed and forgiven.

That, my friend, is the message of Jesus and His supreme love. He came and died and rose to forgive us for all our mistakes. He gave His life so that we can be free to be the mothers we were created to be. There is hope for all mothers and daughters. Love, friendship, and freedom can blossom in any mother-daughter relationship. No mother should try to do it by herself. When she gets in trouble or becomes confused, the star mother has learned where to go for help. She goes to the One who promised that He will never let you down. That person is God. He sent his Son to prove it. He promises that all things are possible with his help.

With God's help you can do it: You can be a successful mother! It's actually very simple. Believe God's promise. Feel God's power. Accept God's grace and get to know the Supreme Model of Love: Jesus Christ. When you do, you, too, will discover the beauty and the love that can exist between every mother and daughter.